The SUMMER *Cookbook*

The SUMMER *Cookbook*

NANETTE NEWMAN

Photography by
Michael Boys

HAMLYN

The author and publishers would like to thank the General
Trading Company for the loan of props used in many of the
photographs.

Photographic Stylist Fiona Pregoff

Illustrations by Elaine Hill

Published 1986 by
Hamlyn Publishing
Bridge House, London Road,
Twickenham, Middlesex, England

ISBN 0 600 32607 1

Set in Monophoto Bembo
by Servis Filmsetting Limited, Manchester

Printed in Spain by Cayfosa. Barcelona.
Dep. Leg. B-3810-1986

CONTENTS

FOREWORD

I am an optimist. I always think summer is going to be wonderful. I imagine the blue, cloudless skies, the house full of roses, delicious meals eaten out of doors, the herb garden blooming, candlelit evenings watching Turner sunsets, lazing in a hammock, friends and family basking in the warmth of an idyllic summer's day . . . As I said, I am an optimist. I'm also a romantic, given to flights of fancy, and during all the summers I've known I've discovered that a few blissful days make up for all the disappointing ones: the blissful ones are the days I remember and I push the others out of my head.

Of course I've spent hours bending over the proverbial hot stove while everyone else was getting a tan; naturally I have despaired when it has rained on my private parades – those well-planned barbecues or surprise birthday parties. I've also experienced the occasional *crise* when those unexpected weekend guests turn up, bringing with them more unexpected guests, and a lot of ferreting around in the fridge has managed (along with some silent cursing), to produce a meal.

But who wants to dwell on the dog days? I certainly don't and nor, I am sure, do you. Instead, let me help you make the entertaining side of summer easier and more enjoyable. Over the years I've learnt many short cuts (most of them acquired the hard way!) and the first rule is that entertaining should be as enjoyable for the cook as it is for the guests. The flush you acquire from a steaming pan is no substitute for a sun tan, and spending long hours in the kitchen, whatever the result, is not as relaxing as sitting in the garden with a good book, or going on a picnic.

So I have put together a Summer Cookbook for those of you who like to entertain and love to hear the praise of the happy guest. I hope it will give you some ideas, some new recipes and tips to help you have a different and wonderful summer.

Still the optimist, I think it's going to be the best yet.

A TASTE OF SUMMER

Food to Go (Anywhere)

Packed food – for hikes, bikes, sight-seeing, boating or for simply
lying in a hammock.

Away From it All

Picnics of the past were splendid affairs – hampers bulging with
china, plates, linen napkins, delicious delicacies; laid out with care
and attention. A far cry from the soggy sandwich. Here are some
ideas for proper picnics, where the food is an important
part of the occasion.

Food by the Water

Food to eat by the pool, by the sea or by a lake.

Summer Weekends

Ideas to make sure you enjoy the weekend as much
as your guests do.

Lazy Summer Sundays

We all long for these. There are some fairly effortless ideas,
some short cuts and a few easy going recipes to make sure you can
enjoy the day.

Dinner Parties

Some menus to spark off your own ideas for summer entertaining.

Rain Stopped Eating

For those days when the outside meal becomes an indoor one. Food
that is very amenable to change.

Midsummer Madness

Summer parties, celebrations, birthdays, anniversaries – some
thoughts on how to make the occasion.

Food
to Go

(Anywhere)

FILLED COTTAGE LOAF

SERVES 6 TO 8

1 cottage loaf
75 g/3 oz butter
EGG AND WATERCRESS FILLING
knob of butter
3 eggs, lightly beaten
bunch of watercress, chopped
2 tablespoons mayonnaise
salt and pepper
TUNA FILLING
1 (198-g/7-oz) can tuna in oil
225 g/8 oz cottage cheese
25 g/1 oz stuffed green olives, sliced
dash of Tabasco sauce
ALFALFA FILLING
½ cup alfalfa sprouts or bean sprouts
100 g/4 oz frozen sweet corn, defrosted
6 radishes, thinly sliced
4 tablespoons mayonnaise

Slice the top-knot off the loaf then cut the base into three even layers. Butter.

For the egg and watercress filling melt the butter in a small non-stick saucepan. Add the eggs and cook over a low heat, stirring continuously, until scrambled. Remove from the heat and cool completely, stir in the chopped watercress, mayonnaise and seasoning. Chill while preparing the other fillings.

For the second filling drain and flake the tuna, then combine with the cottage cheese and olives. Season to taste with Tabasco, salt and pepper, being careful not to add too much Tabasco as it is very hot. Finally make the sweet corn filling by combining all the ingredients and season well.

Sandwich the loaf together with the three fillings. The whole loaf can then be cut into wedges and put back together. Wrap securely in cling film.

STUFFED PITTA BREADS

SERVES 8

Stuffed pittas make ideal picnic food because they travel well.

RICE FILLING
100 g/4 oz brown or white rice
4 tablespoons well-seasoned vinaigrette
100 g/4 oz mozzarella cheese
7.5-cm/3-in piece cucumber
4 tomatoes
a few basil leaves, chopped
salt and pepper
4 pitta breads
ALFALFA FILLING
1 (100-g/4-oz) packet mixed salted nuts
100 g/4 oz alfalfa sprouts
1 dessert apple, cored and chopped
175 g/6 oz smoked applewood cheese, diced
(or your favourite cheese)
4 tablespoons natural yogurt
4 wholewheat pittas

Cook the rice in boiling water until just tender. Drain then stir in the vinaigrette while the rice is still hot. As the mixture cools the rice will absorb the dressing which gives it a good flavour.

Meanwhile slice the cheese, cucumber and tomatoes quite small. When the rice is cold, stir together with the basil and seasoning. Split the pittas along one long edge and carefully open up the pockets. Divide the filling between the pittas, then wrap securely in cling film.

For the second filling, roughly chop the nuts and stir into the sprouts with the apple, cheese and yogurt; season well. Split the pittas down one long side and open up the pockets carefully, then using a spoon divide the filling between them. Wrap individually in cling film.

OUT-IN-THE-COUNTRY PIE

SERVES 6

This tasty pie is easy to cut into slices and it won't lose all its filling en route.

225 g/8 oz plain flour
225 g/8 oz wholemeal flour
salt and pepper
bunch of mixed herbs, including some thyme, a few sprigs of sage and plenty of parsley
225 g/8 oz butter or margarine
about 6 tablespoons cold water
FILLING
225 g/8 oz cooked chicken
100 g/4 oz cooked ham
bunch of spring onions, chopped
225 g/8 oz cottage cheese
freshly grated nutmeg
2 (227-g/8-oz) packets frozen spinach
50 g/2 oz butter, melted
2 eggs, beaten
2 tablespoons double cream
beaten egg to glaze

Mix both types of flour in a bowl, then add a pinch of salt. Chop the herbs. Cut the butter or margarine into pieces and rub it into the flour, then add the herbs and mix well. Stir in enough water to bind the pastry, wrap and chill for a while, then turn out on to a floured surface and knead lightly. Cut about two-thirds off the pastry and set the rest aside. Roll the dough into a circle large enough to line a fairly deep 25-cm/10-in round loose-bottomed flan tin. Press the pastry into the tin, leaving all the excess at the edges. Chill until the filling is ready.

Mince or finely chop the chicken and ham, and put in a bowl. Add the onions, cottage cheese, plenty of seasoning and a generous amount of nutmeg. Cook the spinach accord-ing to the packet instruction and drain thoroughly. Stir in the melted butter, then add the spinach to the chicken mixture. Beat the eggs and cream together and mix everything together. Put this mixture into the pastry case, pressing it down well.

Roll out the reserved pastry into a circle large enough to cover the top of the pie. Lift the pastry on top of the filling, trimming off excess. Brush the very edge of the pastry top with beaten egg, then fold down the edge of the pastry sides to seal the filling in completely. Press the pastry join with a fork to seal it well and make it look attractive. Brush with a little beaten egg and make a small hole in the middle to allow steam to escape.

Bake the pie in a moderately hot oven (200 C, 400 F, gas 6) for 20 minutes, then reduce the oven temperature to moderate (180 C, 350 F, gas 4) and cook for a further 20 minutes. Remove from the oven and leave to cool. While the pie is still warm, loosen it from the sides of the tin by gently lifting the base, then leave to cool completely.

An easy way to remove flans and pies from loose-bottomed tins is to stand the tin on a storage jar, then ease the side down. When cold cut into slices and put back in the shape of the pie, then wrap in cling film for taking on the picnic. It can be made a day or two in advance and stored in the refrigerator.

PORTABLE INSTANT PICNICS

Cut oranges into wedges, then pack them tightly in cling film and chill. Cucumber, melons, grapefruit or pine-apple can also be cut into pieces, re-shaped and packed in this way. Put the packages in bags of ice to keep really cool.

SUNFLOWER DIP

This is so easy the children can make it. Put it in a screw-topped jar, airtight container or one of those wide-necked vacuum flasks and chill thoroughly.

Mix a large handful of sunflower seeds and soy sauce to taste into 150 ml/¼ pint natural yogurt and 150 ml/¼ pint mayonnaise. Blend the mixture in a liquidiser until almost smooth, then add some tarragon.

To eat with the dip, have fresh vegetables – cauliflower, carrots, celery, cucumber, red and green pepper, radicchio, chicory or mange-tout. To make sure that the vegetables stay crunchy when they have been packed for several hours, cut them up in advance and soak in plenty of ice-cold water for a couple of hours. Drain and pack them at the last minute.

Above: Beef and Carrot Loaf (page 17); opposite: Sunflower Dip

ENERGY SNACK

In a large bowl mix together 2 heaped tablespoons oatmeal, 1 heaped tablespoon sunflower seeds, a handful of raisins, some chopped apricots, a handful of nuts (your choice), a handful of malted breakfast cereal, a sprinkling of shredded coconut and about 2 tablespoons honey. Stir the mixture then put it on to a lightly oiled baking tin and bake in a moderate oven (180 C, 350 F, gas 4) for about 20 minutes, stirring often during cooking. Leave to cool before putting in a bag to take on the picnic.

NOTE: Use the energy snack in muffins. Add a large handful to your basic muffin mixture (see page 97) and cook as directed in the recipe. The energy snack also tastes good mixed into natural yogurt.

PARSNIP LOAF

MAKES 1 LARGE LOAF

15 g/½ oz dried yeast
scant 300 ml/½ pint tepid water
1 teaspoon sugar
450 g/1 lb strong plain flour (or half plain, half wholemeal)
2 teaspoons salt
1 onion, finely chopped
100 g/4 oz Gruyère, grated
225 g/8 oz parsnips, cooked and mashed with a large knob of butter
handful of sesame seeds to sprinkle on top

Sprinkle the yeast over the tepid water. Stir in the sugar, then leave in a warm place until frothy.

Put the flour and salt in a bowl, then add the onion and cheese and mix well. Make a well in the middle, add the parsnips and stir in the yeast liquid, then mix in the flour to make a dough. Knead thoroughly for about 10 minutes. You can do this in a food mixer or food processor.

Shape the dough into a thick round loaf and put it on a greased baking tray. Cover with oiled cling film, leave in a warm place until doubled in size, then cut a cross in the top. Brush with a little water and sprinkle with the sesame seeds before baking in a hot oven (230 C, 450 F, gas 8) for about 40 minutes. When the loaf is cooked it will sound hollow when you tap the bottom. Leave to cool on a wire rack.

BEEF AND CARROT LOAF

(Illustrated on page 14)

SERVES 6

1 kg/2 lb minced chuck steak
2 large carrots, coarsely grated
2 onions, chopped · 1 clove garlic, crushed
50 g/2 oz wholemeal breadcrumbs
1 egg, beaten
generous dash of Worcestershire sauce
1 generous tablespoon tomato ketchup
large handful fresh parsley (or mixed fresh herbs), chopped
salt and pepper
1 (225-g/8-oz) packet frozen chopped spinach, drained
freshly grated nutmeg
450 g/1 lb cottage cheese

Mix the beef with the carrots, onions, garlic, breadcrumbs and the egg. Add the Worcestershire sauce, and ketchup, about half the herbs and seasoning. Mix well.

Grease a double-thick piece of cooking foil. Turn the meat out on to this and pat it flat into an evenly thick oblong layer measuring roughly 30 × 20 cm/12 × 8 in.

Mix the remaining herbs with the spinach, seasoning and nutmeg. Spoon this down the middle of the beef and carrot mixture, leaving a clear edge at each side. Spoon the cottage cheese down the middle of the spinach. Flip the long edges of the foil so that the meat folds over the filling. Pinch the edges together. Place the baking tin beside the foil and gently lift one side and roll the whole loaf on to the tray (it should land with the seamed side down).

Bake in a moderate oven (180 C, 350 F, gas 4) for 1 hour 50 minutes. Open the foil and leave the loaf to cool before slicing and packing it in cling film ready to take on the picnic.

SESAME CRACKERS

MAKES ABOUT 16

225 g/8 oz wholewheat semolina
100 g/4 oz wholemeal flour
1 teaspoon ground coriander
1 teaspoon grated nutmeg
100 g/4 oz butter
50 g/2 oz sesame seeds
1 egg, beaten
about 50 ml/2 fl oz water
1 tablespoon coarse sea salt
extra sesame seeds to sprinkle over the crackers

Mix the semolina with the flour and spices in a bowl. Rub in the butter until the mixture is like fine breadcrumbs, then stir in the sesame seeds. Add the egg and about half the water, mix in the dry ingredients to make a stiff dough, adding more water as needed.

Turn the dough out on to a floured surface and knead it gently, then roll it out into a large thin 25-cm/10-in square. Cut the dough into about 16 squares – more if you want to make the crackers smaller – then press the crackers on greased baking trays to make them thin and sprinkle with coarse salt and sesame seeds. Press the salt lightly into the dough and bake the crackers in a moderate oven (180 C, 350 F, gas 4) for about 8 to 10 minutes. Leave on the trays briefly, then transfer to a wire rack to cool completely.

CHEESE AND PARSLEY BISCUITS

MAKES 12

These are so good eaten with apples and cheese.

100 g/4 oz wholemeal flour
50 g/2 oz medium oatmeal
pinch of salt
75 g/3 oz sunflower margarine
75 g/3 oz cheese, grated
bunch of parsley, chopped

Mix the flour with the oatmeal and a generous pinch of salt. Add the margarine, cut it into pieces then rub it into the dry ingredients. Stir in the cheese and parsley. Knead the mixture together to form a dough. Alternatively, mix all the ingredients in a food processor.

Roll out on a lightly floured surface and cut out 12 biscuits. Place on greased baking trays and bake in a moderate oven (180 C, 350 F, gas 4) for 20 to 25 minutes.

Leave the biscuits on the trays for a few minutes, then transfer them to a wire rack to cool completely.

Left to right: Energy Cookies, Chocolate and Walnut Shortbread and Muesli Biscuits (all on page 21)

CARAWAY SLICES

MAKES 20

225 g/8 oz wholemeal flour
pinch of salt
75 g/3 oz sunflower margarine or butter
75 g/3 oz Cheddar cheese, grated
1 teaspoon caraway seeds
1 onion
1 egg yolk

Put the flour and salt in a bowl, then rub in the margarine or butter. Stir in the cheese and caraway seeds. Grate the onion and drain off the juice, add to the mixture. Stir in the egg yolk to make a dough. Alternatively, you can make it in a food processor.

Shape the dough into a roll measuring about 20 cm/8 in long and wrap in cling film. Chill in the refrigerator for 30 to 40 minutes or in the freezer for about 15 minutes, until the dough is really firm. Cut the roll into 20 slices and place these slightly apart on greased baking trays.

Bake in a moderately hot oven (200 C, 400 F, gas 6) for 15 to 20 minutes or until golden brown. Leave on the tray for a few minutes then transfer the biscuits to a wire rack to cool completely.

SPICED DATE COOKIES

MAKES 16

100 g/4 oz butter
50 g/2 oz caster sugar
175 g/6 oz plain flour
1 teaspoon ground mixed spice
grated rind of 2 oranges
grated rind of 2 lemons
50 g/2 oz dates, chopped
2 tablespoons brandy or rum
50 g/2 oz walnuts, chopped

Cream the butter with the sugar until the mixture is pale and soft. Mix the flour with the spice, then add to the creamed mixture with the orange and lemon rind, dates and brandy. Mix well to form a soft dough.

Roll the mixture out on a floured surface then cut out 16 biscuits and place them slightly apart on greased baking trays. Flatten the biscuits with a fork, then press some walnuts on top of each. Bake in a moderately hot oven (190 C, 375 F, gas 5) for 15 to 20 minutes or until golden brown. Leave on the tray for a minute, then transfer the biscuits to a wire rack to cool completely.

CHOCOLATE AND WALNUT SHORTBREAD

(Illustrated on page 19)

MAKES 12

175 g/6 oz butter · 75 g/3 oz caster sugar
250 g/9 oz plain flour
100 g/4 oz walnuts, chopped
100 g/4 oz chocolate drops

Cream the butter and sugar until very pale them mix in the flour, walnuts and chocolate drops. When well combined, lightly press the mixture into a greased oblong tin measuring about 23 × 33 cm/ 9 × 13 in.

Bake the shortbread in a moderate oven (180 C, 350 F, gas 4) for 30 minutes until golden. Leave for a few minutes, cut into pieces and leave to cool.

ENERGY COOKIES

(Illustrated on page 19)

MAKES 20

175 g/6 oz plain flour
½ teaspoon ground cinnamon
grated rind of 1 orange
25 g/1 oz icing sugar · 100 g/4 oz butter
2 carrots, coarsely grated
large handful each of sunflower seeds and raisins

Mix the flour, cinnamon, orange rind and icing sugar. Rub in the butter. Mix in the remaining ingredients.

Roughly divide the mixture into 20 portions, then roll each into a ball and place them slightly apart on greased baking trays. Flatten into circles and bake in a moderately hot oven (200 C, 400 F, gas 6) for 15 to 20 minutes or until golden brown. Leave on the trays for a minute, then transfer them to a wire rack to cool completely.

MUESLI BISCUITS

MAKES 16

These are the easiest biscuits to make and deliciously chewy to eat. Home-made muesli with plenty of fruit and nuts is best.

225 g/8 oz butter
225 g/8 oz clear honey
100 g/4 oz demerara sugar
225 g/8 oz muesli
225 g/8 oz rolled oats

Melt the butter with the honey and sugar then thoroughly mix in the muesli and oats. Put spoonfuls on to a greased baking tray.

Bake the biscuits in a moderate oven (180 C, 350 F, gas 4) for 30 minutes. Leave to cool on the tray for a few minutes before transferring to wire racks to cool completely.

NOTE: If you like the mixture can be pressed into a greased shallow oblong baking tin, then cut into fingers when cold. *(Illustrated on page 19)*

POPPY SEED POUND CAKE

MAKES AN 18-CM/7-IN CAKE

225 g/8 oz butter
225 g/8 oz caster sugar
grated rind of 1 lemon
4 eggs
225 g/8 oz self-raising flour
½ teaspoon ground cinnamon
100 g/4 oz poppy seeds
2 tablespoons milk

Cream the butter with the sugar and lemon rind until soft and pale. Add the eggs, then add the flour and cinnamon, then the poppy seeds, gently folding everything in. Lastly add the milk.

Line and grease an 18-cm/7-in deep round cake tin. Turn the mixture into the tin and bake in a moderate oven (160 C, 325 F, gas 3) for 1½ hours. Check the cake towards the end of the cooking time and if it looks very brown on top cover with a piece of cooking foil.

Turn the cake out on to a wire rack to cool. Sprinkle the top with a little caster sugar while still hot.

Peach and Almond Cake (page 24)

PEACH AND ALMOND CAKE

(Illustrated on previous page)

SERVES 12

Demerara sugar and chopped toasted almonds give this cake a wonderfully crunchy crust.

175 g/6 oz butter or margarine
175 g/6 oz caster sugar
grated rind of 1 orange
3 eggs
175 g/6 oz self-raising flour
100 g/4 oz ground almonds
100 g/4 oz dried peaches (some may need soaking), chopped (or use ordinary dried apricots, soaked overnight and thoroughly drained)
150 g/5 oz blanched almonds, chopped
2 tablespoons orange juice
2 tablespoons demerara sugar

Cream the butter or margarine with the sugar and orange rind until pale and very soft, then beat in the eggs. Mix the flour, ground almonds, peach and most of the chopped nuts (save a small handful for the top of the cake), then fold these ingredients into the cake. Add the orange juice, stirring very gently, to soften the mixture.

Turn the mixture into a lined and greased 20-cm/8-in round deep cake tin, then sprinkle the demerara sugar and remaining nuts on top. Bake in a moderate oven (160 C, 325 F, gas 3) for 1½ hours. Turn the cake out on to a wire rack to cool.

HAZELNUT COOKIES

MAKES ABOUT 24

225 g/8 oz butter
175 g/6 oz soft brown sugar
175 g/6 oz caster sugar
2 eggs, beaten
1 teaspoon vanilla essence
250 g/9 oz self-raising flour
1 teaspoon baking powder
1 teaspoon bicarbonate of soda
½ teaspoon ground cinnamon or ground mixed spice
175 g/6 oz hazelnuts, toasted and chopped

Beat the butter and sugars together until they are soft and creamy, then gradually beat in the eggs and vanilla. Mix the flour with the baking powder, bicarbonate of soda and salt, then gently stir these dry ingredients into the creamed mixture. Lastly, stir in the nuts.

Place spoonfuls of the mixture well apart on greased baking trays. Bake in a moderate oven (180 C, 350 F, gas 4) for about 10 to 12 minutes until pale brown. Leave on the trays for a few minutes before transferring them to wire racks to cool completely. Keep making batches until the mixture is used up.

LUMPY BUNS

MAKES 14

These are as easy to make as old-fashioned rock cakes but they taste much nicer.

225 g/8 oz Granary flour
2 teaspoons baking powder
100 g/4 oz butter, cut into small pieces
handful of cracked wheat
50 g/2 oz rye flakes
75 g/3 oz currants
grated rind of 1 orange
2 tablespoons chopped crystallised fruit
25 g/1 oz desiccated coconut
50 g/2 oz demerara sugar
1 teaspoon ground mixed spice
2 eggs, beaten

Put the flour and baking powder in a bowl, then add the butter and rub it in. Alternatively, put the ingredients in a food processor and process until fine. Stir in the cracked wheat, rye flakes and currants. Add the orange rind, crystallised fruit, coconut, sugar and spice, then mix really well. Stir in the eggs to make a fairly firm mixture.

Take spoonfuls of the mixture (there is enough to make 14 buns) and place them slightly apart on greased baking trays. Bake in a moderately hot oven (200 C, 400 F, gas 6) for 15 minutes or until risen and golden. Cool on wire racks.

NOTE: You can bake these in greased muffin pans.

BASIC HOME-MADE LEMONADE

SERVES 8

pared rind and juice of 6 lemons
1.15 litres/2 pints water
honey to taste
several sprigs of lemon balm

Put the lemon rind and juice in a saucepan and pour in the water. Add some honey, bring to the boil, then remove from the heat and add the herb sprigs. Leave to cool slightly before adding more honey to taste. Stir, then leave to cool completely. Strain and chill.

NOTE: If you like, pulverise chopped lemons with sugar, pour boiling water over them and leave until cold. Pour through a sieve.

TOMATO COOLER

SERVES 4

900 ml/1½ pints tomato juice
juice of ½ lemon
a little grated lemon rind
generous dash of Tabasco sauce
generous dash of Worcestershire sauce
plenty of ice
a few sprigs of mint

Mix all the ingredients and pour into a vacuum flask to carry on the picnic. Alternatively, thoroughly chill the drink, pour it into a bottle and put this in a chiller box to keep cool.

Away From it All

(But taking it with you)

SALAD IN A LOAF

SERVES 6

1 wholemeal sandwich loaf
75 g / 3 oz butter
450 g / 1 lb cooked ham in one piece
6 hard-boiled eggs
2 tablespoons capers
175 g / 6 oz tiny shelled broad beans (blanched
briefly if you think they need it)
bunch of chives, chopped
50 g / 2 oz stoned black olives, chopped
DRESSING
300 ml / ½ pint mayonnaise
1 tablespoon mustard with horseradish
2 teaspoons chopped tarragon
pinch of sugar · salt and pepper
1 clove garlic, crushed (optional)
a few drops of lemon juice

Thinly slice all the crusts off the loaf. Horizontally slice a lid off the bread, then cut out all the middle of the loaf leaving about 2.5 cm / 1 in of bread all round the sides and base to make a box shape. You can freeze the bread which is removed from inside the loaf to make breadcrumbs.

Melt the butter, then brush the loaf and the lid all over, both inside and out. Put the bread on a baking tray and bake in a moderately hot oven (200 C, 400 F, gas 6) for about 20 minutes or until crisp and browned. Leave to cool.

Cut the ham into cubes. Quarter the eggs and mix them with the ham, capers, beans, chives and olives. Lightly toss the ingredients, then put the salad in a plastic bag and put this inside the crisp loaf and put the lid on top. Wrap the whole loaf in foil or cling film and chill it until you are ready to leave.

Mix all the ingredients for the dressing in a container with a tight-fitting lid. Chill. When you arrive simply turn the salad out of the bag into the loaf crust and pour the dressing on the salad. Eat with some of the container loaf.

THREE-MELON SALAD

(Illustrated on back cover)

SERVES 6 TO 8

1 watermelon
1 honeydew melon
1 charentais melon
lemon balm or pineapple mint (if you have it)
1 (227-g / 8-oz) can lychees, drained

Cut a slice off the top of the watermelon to make a lid. Scoop out all the flesh and cut it into chunks, discarding the seeds. Put the watermelon flesh in a bowl. Halve the honeydew, discard the seeds, then scoop out the flesh and mix it with the watermelon. Do the same with the charentais. (You can use a melon baller for this.)

Add the sprigs of lemon balm or mint and lychees to the melon mixture. Fill the watermelon shell with the melon and wrap it securely in a couple of thicknesses of cling film.

Pack the melon in plenty of ice and it will keep cold for several hours. This is best in a chiller box, otherwise put some ice in a very thick plastic bag, and put the completely sealed melon on top before sealing the bag.

MINTED CUCUMBER MOUSSE

(Illustrated overleaf)

SERVES 6

$\frac{1}{2}$ *cucumber, lightly peeled and diced*
salt and pepper
15 g/$\frac{1}{2}$ oz gelatine
150 ml/$\frac{1}{4}$ pint hot chicken stock
large bunch of mint
1 tablespoon white wine vinegar (or cider vinegar)
1$\frac{1}{2}$ teaspoons caster sugar
pinch of ground coriander or mace
225 g/8 oz cream cheese
150 ml/$\frac{1}{4}$ pint double cream
2 egg whites

Put the cucumber in a sieve or colander over a bowl and sprinkle it with salt, then set aside for 30 minutes. Soften the gelatine in a little cold water, then dissolve in the stock and leave until almost cold.

Chop some of the mint to flavour the mousse. Dry the cucumber. Mix it with the vinegar, sugar, coriander or mace and mint. Beat cheese, adding stock gradually. Then add cucumber. Stir well and leave until beginning to set.

Whip the cream until it is just thick, then fold it into the mousse. Whisk the egg whites until stiff, fold them in and pour into a 23-cm/9-in ring mould. Chill until set.

Wrap the mould completely in cling film or foil to carry on the picnic. Turn it out and fill the middle with watercress or alfalfa sprouts or cucumber.

CHICKEN STRIPS

SERVES 6

2 chicken breast fillets
salt and pepper
a little flour
100 g/4 oz dry breadcrumbs
bunch of parsley, chopped
grated rind of 1 lime or lemon
1 egg, beaten
oil for deep frying
TO SERVE
halved lemons

Cut the chicken into fine strips. Season the flour fairly generously, then coat the pieces of chicken in it. Mix the breadcrumbs with the parsley and lime or lemon rind. Put the mixture on a deep plate.

Dip the floured chicken strips in the egg, then roll them in the breadcrumb mixture to coat them completely. Lay a piece of greaseproof paper on a baking tray and put the chicken on it, then (if you have time) put the tray in the freezer for about 15 to 30 minutes.

Heat the oil for deep frying to 190 c/375 f. Drop the chicken strips in the oil and cook until crisp and golden. Drain thoroughly on absorbent kitchen paper and leave to cool.

To pack the chicken, line a container with some absorbent kitchen paper and put the strips on top. Put lemon halves in the corners and place an airtight lid on top. Or completely wrap in cling film or foil.

RUNNER BEAN SALAD

Slice some fresh runner beans and remove any tough strings. Blanch them very briefly in boiling water, then plunge them into ice cold water. Drain thoroughly. Mix the beans with freshly ground black pepper and a squeeze of lemon juice for the best flavour.

Above: Chicken and Grapes (overleaf); opposite: Minted Cucumber Mousse (page 29) with Sandwich Loaf (page 33)

STUFFED MANGE-TOUT

SERVES 6

about 20 mange-tout
FILLING
100 g/4 oz cream cheese
1 tablespoon natural yogurt
salt and pepper
a few spring onions, chopped
50 g/2 oz peeled cooked prawns, finely chopped
2 teaspoons tomato purée

Blend all the filling ingredients together. Gently open the mange-tout pods down one side and fill with the mixture. Pack in a container lined with mint.

NOTE: Steam the mange-tout if you prefer.

CHICKEN AND GRAPES

(Illustrated on previous page)

SERVES 4

4 small melons · 4 chicken breasts, poached
25 g/1 oz sliced blanched almonds, toasted
bunch of spring onions, chopped
225 g/8 oz seedless white grapes
250 ml/8 fl oz mayonnaise
salt and pepper · chopped mint

Cut the tops off the melons and reserve these lids. Scoop out and discard the seeds, then scoop out the melon flesh

and cut it into chunks. Cut the chicken into pieces and mix with all the other ingredients together in a big bowl, adding enough mint to flavour but not overpower the salad.

Dry the insides of the melons with absorbent kitchen paper, then fill them with salad and replace the lids. Stick sprigs of mint into the lids if you like and wrap the melons completely in cling film to keep the lids firmly in place. Chill thoroughly before taking on the picnic.

NOTE: This is a great way of making a wonderful chicken salad which can travel and be served in its own container.

STUFFED COURGETTES IN LETTUCE LEAVES

SERVES 4

4 medium courgettes
salt and pepper
FILLING
100 g/4 oz cream cheese
1 ripe dessert pear, peeled, cored and chopped
about 8 radishes, trimmed and chopped
a couple of spring onions, chopped
2 tablespoons chopped tarragon
4-8 lettuce leaves

Trim the courgettes, then cut them in half lengthways and scoop out the seeds. Blanch the courgette halves very briefly in boiling salted water, then drain them thoroughly on absorbent kitchen paper.

Beat the cream cheese, add the pear and radishes. Add the spring onions and tarragon with seasoning to taste. Sandwich the courgette halves back together with the filling, then wrap them in one or two lettuce leaves. Pack the courgettes in a container on ice.

SANDWICH LOAF

(Illustrated on page 30)

SERVES 6 TO 8

Some sandwiches are definitely boring – here is a way of making a sandwich into something special.

1 wholemeal sandwich loaf
225 g/8 oz cooked ham
300 ml/½ pint mayonnaise
2 teaspoons green peppercorns (optional)
225 g/8 oz cooked chicken
a few spring onions, chopped
350 g/12 oz cream cheese
large bunch of mixed fresh herbs, chopped

Cut all the crusts off the bread to leave an oblong-shaped loaf, then cut this through horizontally into seven slices. Blend the ham with half the mayonnaise in a liquidiser or food processor until smooth then stir in the peppercorns. In the same way, blend the remaining mayonnaise with the chicken and add the spring onions. Beat the cream cheese with the herbs.

Sandwich the slices of bread together with the three separate fillings so that there are two layers of each. Pack the loaf tightly in cling film and chill it thoroughly.

The loaf should be cut vertically into slices, then reshaped and packed securely in cling film ready to take on the picnic. The slices can be cut across into fingers to make them easier to eat if you like.

Alternative Fillings
Drained canned tuna and chopped hard-boiled egg and some chopped spring onions in mayonnaise (for one layer). Finely chopped watercress and cream cheese (for the next layer). Grated carrot, sultanas and mayonnaise (for the third layer).

PICNIC CROISSANTS

MAKES 12

Instead of sandwiches, try filling wholemeal croissants with unusual mixtures.

12 croissants (page 96)
CARROT AND NECTARINE FILLING
3–4 carrots, grated
2 nectarines, halved, stoned and chopped
50 g/2 oz walnuts, chopped
salt and pepper
a few drops of lemon juice
4 tablespoons mayonnaise
SUNFLOWER AND CRESS FILLING
1 carton mustard and cress
handful of sunflower seeds, lightly toasted
1 small red onion, sliced into thin rings
1 dessert apple, cored and diced
a few drops of lemon juice
2 tablespoons soured cream

Make the croissants if you have the time, otherwise buy them from a good baker. The fat crunchy ones are best.

Mix the carrots with the nectarines and walnuts, then add seasoning to taste and sprinkle with lemon juice. Mix in the mayonnaise.

For the second filling, mix the cress with the sunflower seeds and onion. Sprinkle the apple with lemon juice and toss well with the mustard and cress. Mix with soured cream and season to taste.

Split the croissants through and fill them with the fillings, then wrap each one in cling film to keep them whole.

WHITE CABBAGE SALAD

For a delicious, simple-to-prepare salad, mix shredded white cabbage with shredded chicory leaves and finely sliced green pepper. Sprinkle a few caraway seeds over the salad and dress it with mayonnaise thinned with a little single cream or with a vinaigrette dressing if you prefer.

CABBAGE WITH KUMQUAT DRESSING

Poach 50 g/2 oz kumquats in 4 tablespoons water and 2 tablespoons red wine vinegar for about 10 minutes, or until tender. Keep the pan covered to retain all the moisture.

Put the kumquats with the cooking liquid in a food processor or liquidiser with the juice of 1 lemon and 150 ml/$\frac{1}{4}$ pint sunflower oil. Add seasoning to taste and blend until smooth and thick. Stir in 2 tablespoons chopped fresh marjoram and 1 tablespoon finely chopped shallot or onion.

Pour the dressing over finely shredded white or red cabbage just before it is served.

Vegetable Terrine (overleaf)

VEGETABLE TERRINE

(Illustrated on previous page)

SERVES 6 TO 8

100 g/4 oz butter
75 g/3 oz plain flour
600 ml/1 pint milk
2 eggs, beaten
225 g/8 oz carrots, chopped
1 onion, chopped
salt and pepper
225 g/8 oz ricotta cheese
bunch of watercress, trimmed
½ cauliflower, lightly cooked
75 g/3 oz white cheese (Lancashire, Caerphilly or Cheshire), crumbled
225 g/8 oz shelled peas, cooked
some chopped mint

Line the base of a 1-kg/2-lb loaf tin with greaseproof paper and grease well. Melt 75 g/3 oz of the butter in a saucepan, stir in the flour then gradually add the milk and bring to the boil, stirring all the time. Remove from the heat and beat in the eggs, set aside.

Cook the carrots and onion in the remaining butter until the onion is soft. Stir in a quarter of the sauce then put into a liquidiser or food processor and blend until smooth. Add seasoning to taste, then turn the mixture into the prepared tin and smooth the top down well.

Blend the ricotta cheese with the watercress and one-third of the remaining sauce. Season and pour the mixture into the tin, pressing down lightly to make an even layer.

Break the cauliflower into small pieces and blend these with the cheese and half the remaining sauce until smooth. Season and turn into the tin to form the third layer, spreading it out evenly.

Finally, blend the peas and mint with the remaining sauce until smooth. Spread this mixture evenly over the cauliflower layer. Stand the terrine in a roasting tin half filled with boiling water. Bake in a moderate oven (160 C, 325 F, gas 3) for 1½ hours. Leave until completely cold and chill for a few hours before wrapping the whole tin in a double thickness of foil. Turn the terrine out just before you serve it. Garnish with herbs.

NOTE: If you don't have a chiller box to carry your food in, put as many ice cubes as you can in a dustbin bag, place your containers (well-sealed with foil or cling film) in the bag and tie it very securely. This helps to keep food in good condition. Take the food out carefully and the water might be useful for sticky fingers.

WHOLE ARTICHOKES VINAIGRETTE

These are easy to pack and carry on a picnic, with the dressing in a screw-topped jar to pour over the vegetables at the last minute.

To cook artichokes, simply trim the ends of the leaves and put them in boiling salted water – they take about 15 to 20 minutes depending on size and age. Drain and rinse in cold water, then pull out the hairy choke from the middle to leave the outer leaves and the bottom in place. Cool, wrap tightly in cling film and chill.

Make a well-flavoured vinaigrette dressing, with oil of your choice, cider vinegar or wine vinegar, a pinch of sugar and seasoning, some mustard, a crushed clove of garlic and 2 tablespoons chopped chervil or dill. Shake up the dressing just before you use it.

PINEAPPLE AND MANGO SALAD

BAKED SALMON

SERVES 8 TO 10

1 (2.25-kg/5-lb) salmon or salmon trout
50 g/2 oz butter
150 ml/¼ pint dry white wine
bay leaf
bunch of dill sprigs
a few sprigs of tarragon
small bunch of parsley
salt and pepper
dill sprigs to garnish

Peel and core a large ripe pineapple, then cut into chunks. Peel 3 ripe mangos and cut the flesh off the stones in thin slices. Cut these in half and mix with the pineapple in a container which has a tight-fitting lid. Sprinkle in a few tablespoons of white rum and a little icing sugar if you like. If you have any, a couple of tablespoons of coconut liqueur taste good sprinkled over the fruit but you will definitely have to omit the sugar with this. Chill thoroughly before taking on the picnic.

NOTE: When tiny pineapples are available, use one per person and cut off the tops. Scoop out the insides and chop the fruit. Mix with thinly sliced kiwi fruit and put back into the pineapple. Put the lid back on top and chill before serving.

Ask the fishmonger to clean the fish for you. Take a large, double-thick piece of cooking foil and lay it on a roasting tin – there should be plenty to wrap the salmon. Butter the middle of the foil, put the salmon on it and dot with the remaining butter.

Cup the sides of the foil, sprinkle the wine over the salmon and add the bay leaf. Roughly chop the other herbs and sprinkle over the fish. Add a little seasoning and wrap up securely in the foil.

Bake in a moderate oven (160 C, 325 F, gas 3) for about 1½ hours. Check that the salmon is cooked through, then wrap it tightly and leave to cool. Remove the skin from head to tail and wrap the salmon in fresh foil. Add a few sprigs of dill and chill. Serve with home-made mayonnaise (see page 41).

STRAWBERRY COEUR À LA CRÈME

Take a basket of strawberries to serve with traditional coeur à la crème. Make the coeur à la crème by beating a little cream taken from $150\,ml/\frac{1}{4}$ pint double cream into $225\,g/8\,oz$ cream cheese. Whip the remaining cream with a couple of tablespoons of icing sugar, then fold it into the cream cheese. Whisk an egg white until stiff and fold in. Spoon the mixture into muslin-lined coeur à la crème moulds and stand them on a plate or dish in the refrigerator. Leave overnight, then pack the drained coeur à la crème moulds in cling film and put in a chiller box. Turn them out on the picnic and have with the strawberries.

Gooseberry Flan with Cashew and Coriander Shortbread (both overleaf)

GOOSEBERRY FLAN

(Illustrated on previous page)

SERVES 6 TO 8

150 g/5 oz wholemeal flour
150 g/5 oz plain flour
175 g/6 oz butter
75 g/3 oz toasted hazelnuts, ground
2 tablespoons demerara sugar
about 3 tablespoons water
GINGER CREAM FILLING
25 g/1 oz cornflour
15 g/½ oz caster sugar
300 ml/½ pint milk
1 vanilla pod, split
2 egg yolks
2 pieces preserved stem ginger, chopped
2 tablespoons ginger syrup (from the preserved ginger)
1 egg white
GOOSEBERRY FILLING
1 kg/2 lb gooseberries
100 g/4 oz sugar
150 ml/¼ pint water
15 g/½ oz gelatine

Mix the flours in a bowl, rub in the butter then add the nuts and sugar. Stir in just enough water to bind the ingredients and mix them together to form a dough. Roll out the pastry and use to line an oblong tin measuring about 8½ × 12 in/ 21 × 30 cm. Prick the base all over with a fork and lay a piece of greaseproof paper on top. Sprinkle in dried peas or beans and bake the pastry case in a moderately hot oven (200 C, 400 F, gas 6) for 10 minutes. Remove the greaseproof paper and peas or beans then bake for a further 5 to 10 minutes or until brown and crisp. Leave to cool.

To make the ginger cream filling, mix the cornflour and caster sugar to a smooth paste with a little of the milk. Bring the remaining milk to the boil with the vanilla pod, leave to infuse for 10 minutes, then strain the milk on to the cornflour mixture. Pour the mixture back into the saucepan and bring to the boil, stirring all the time. Cook for 2 minutes then remove from the heat and beat in the egg yolks, ginger and syrup. Leave until cool.

Top and tail the gooseberries. Dissolve the sugar in the water, then poach the fruit in this syrup for 1 to 2 minutes until just softened but still whole. Soften the gelatine in a little cold water. Off the heat, add the gelatine to the gooseberries and stir until it dissolves. Cool.

To finish the ginger cream, whisk the egg white until stiff and fold it into the cream. Spread this in the pastry case, then top with the gooseberries. Chill until completely set. Wrap securely in a double thickness of foil.

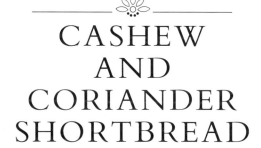

CASHEW AND CORIANDER SHORTBREAD

(Illustrated on previous page)

MAKES 24

100 g/4 oz butter · 50 g/2 oz caster sugar
150 g/5 oz plain flour · 25 g/1 oz rice flour
100 g/4 oz cashew nuts, ground
coarsely grated rind of 2 large oranges
3 teaspoons ground coriander

Cream the butter with the sugar until very soft and pale, then mix in the flour, rice flour, cashew nuts, orange rind and coriander. Press the mixture into a greased 20-cm/8-in square tin and bake in a moderate oven (180 C, 350 F, gas 4) for 1 hour.

Cut the shortbread into pieces and leave them in the tin for 5 minutes before carefully lifting them on to a wire rack to cool.

APPLE CAKE

SERVES 10

450 g / 1 lb cooking apples
450 g / 1 lb self-raising flour
3 teaspoons baking powder
½ teaspoon ground cinnamon
50 g / 2 oz walnuts
grated rind of 1 orange
grated rind of 1 lemon
225 g / 8 oz caster sugar
100 ml / 4 fl oz sunflower oil
3 eggs

Peel and core the apples, then cut into chunks. Sift the flour with the baking powder and cinnamon. Chop the walnuts with the apples in a food processor until finely chopped but not slushy. Add the orange and lemon rind.

Beat the sugar, oil and eggs together until light and fluffy. Fold in the dry ingredients, then fold in the apple and nut mixture. Turn into a greased 25-cm / 10-in springform tin and bake in a moderate oven (180 C, 350 F, gas 4) for 1¾ hours. Turn out and cool the cake on a wire rack.

NOTE: Serve the cake with whipped cream flavoured with a dash of Calvados, or cream mixed with thick apple purée.

HOME-MADE MAYONNAISE

Home-made mayonnaise is by far the best. Whisk 2 egg yolks with a pinch of dry mustard and seasoning. Add a little lemon juice and a few drops of oil and whisk thoroughly until well combined. Whisking all the time, gradually add 250 ml / 8 fl oz oil, pouring it in drop by drop. When the mixture is very creamy add lemon juice to taste and a pinch of sugar if you like. Chill lightly.

IDEAS FOR PICNICS

Buy flowered sheets in the sales and use as picnic tablecloths. (If you buy the pillow cases as well you can take matching pillows to sit on.)

Always take mosquito spray and sting cream, also food covers (the best ones are umbrella shaped and open out quite large).

Pack face cloths soaked in cold water scented with cologne and pack in ice-filled polythene bags.

Take sun hats and (dare I say it) a large umbrella.

Food by the Water

(I do like to
eat beside
the seaside...
or lake...
or pool)

COLD TOMATO SOUP WITH BASIL

SERVES 4

1 kg/2 lb ripe tomatoes
½ teaspoon sugar
1 tablespoon chopped basil
150 ml/¼ pint single cream
1 teaspoon Tabasco sauce
salt and pepper

Put the tomatoes into a bowl, pour on boiling water and leave for a minute. Drain, peel and remove the seeds. Put the tomatoes in a liquidiser or food processor and add all the other ingredients. Purée until smooth, then chill thoroughly before serving.

Alternatively, put the tomato purée in the freezer, freeze until slushy, then whisk thoroughly and re-freeze until firm. Serve scooped into dishes.

TUNA AND OLIVE SALAD

SERVES 6

Served with crusty bread and its own tangy dressing this salad takes only minutes to prepare.

3 (198-g/7-oz) cans tuna in oil
2 green or yellow peppers
4 hard-boiled eggs
bunch of spring onions, chopped
50 g/2 oz black olives, stoned
4 tablespoons chopped parsley
150 ml/¼ pint natural yogurt and mayonnaise (mixed)
lemon juice
black pepper

Drain and flake the tuna reserving the oil for the dressing. Cut the stalk ends off the peppers, remove any seeds and pith, then thinly slice. Chop the eggs then combine with the tuna, peppers, spring onions, black olives and parsley.

To make the dressing whisk the yogurt with the reserved oil and lemon juice to taste. Season with black pepper. Keep the salad and dressing separate, covered with cling film or packed in a container in the refrigerator or chiller box. Dress the salad just before serving.

STILTON AND WALNUT DRUMSTICKS

SERVES 4

8 chicken drumsticks
about 50 g/2 oz butter
salt and pepper
4 bay leaves
sprigs of fresh rosemary
DRESSING
225 g/8 oz blue Stilton cheese
4–6 tablespoons port
4 tablespoons mayonnaise
225 g/8 oz walnuts, finely chopped
150 ml/¼ pint soured cream
2 lettuce hearts, divided into leaves, to serve

Put the drumsticks in a roasting tin with the butter dotted on top. Sprinkle with salt and pepper, then put the bay leaves and rosemary in between the drumsticks. Cook in a moderately hot oven (200 C, 400 F, gas 6) for about 30 to 45 minutes. When cooked the drumsticks should be quite well browned. Drain them on absorbent kitchen paper and allow to cool.

For the dressing, crumble the cheese, then mash it with the port and mayonnaise. Add the walnuts and stir in the soured cream. Taste and adjust the seasoning; chill the dressing.

To serve, arrange the drumsticks on the leaves from lettuce hearts (this enables you to pick up the drumsticks in a lettuce leaf). Serve the dressing separately.

SAVOURY PHILO BAKE

SERVES 6

175 g/6 oz Gruyère cheese
2 medium courgettes
2 tablespoons chopped fresh basil
bunch of spring onions, chopped
salt and pepper
8 sheets philo pastry
50 g/2 oz butter, melted

Grate the Gruyère and the courgettes, then mix in the basil, onions and seasoning.

Lay the philo pastry on the work surface brushing each sheet with melted butter as you stack them up.

Spread the filling over the top of the pastry stack, leaving a border, then fold the edges over so that they overlap in the middle. Press together to seal in the filling.

Put on a greased baking tray and brush with more butter. Cook in a moderately hot oven (200 C, 400 F, gas 6) for 20 to 30 minutes. Serve hot or cold.

FRUITY CURRIED MACARONI

SERVES 4 TO 6

175 g/6 oz short-cut macaroni
salt and pepper
350 g/12 oz cooked ham · 3 ripe peaches
3 large dessert apples · juice of 1 lemon
1 small red or white onion
50 g/2 oz roasted almonds
DRESSING
1 tablespoon grated fresh root ginger
1 small onion, chopped · 25 g/1 oz butter
3–4 teaspoons curry powder
4 tablespoons each of soured cream and
mayonnaise
3 tablespoons mango chutney (optional)

Cook the macaroni in boiling salted water for about 10 minutes or until *just* tender, then drain it thoroughly and rinse in cold water. Leave to drain.

Cut the ham into strips and mix with the macaroni. Put the peaches in a large bowl, cover them with boiling water and leave for about a minute. Remove and use a sharp pointed knife to remove the skin. Cut into slices. Add the peaches to the macaroni.

Core and slice the apples (dip in lemon juice), cut the onion into thin slices and add both to the salad, then toss in the almonds. Make the dressing: cook the ginger and onion in the butter until the onion is soft but not browned. Stir in the curry powder and cook gently for a further 3 to 4 minutes, stirring to prevent it from sticking. Press firmly through a sieve so that you get all the juice and flavour without the bits. Fold into the soured cream and mayonnaise. (You can add mango chutney at this point.) Pour the dressing over the salad, toss well and put it in the refrigerator until it is served.

ROQUEFORT EGG MOUSSE

SERVES 6 TO 8

9 eggs
50 g/2 oz butter
50 g/2 oz plain flour
salt and pepper
300 ml/½ pint milk
150 ml/¼ pint double cream
225 g/8 oz Roquefort cheese
handful of chives, chopped
4 teaspoons gelatine
4 tablespoons water
watercress to garnish

Hard-boil 6 eggs, separate the others. Melt the butter in a saucepan, stir in the flour and seasoning and cook for a minute or so. Pour in the milk, stirring all the time, and bring to the boil, still stirring. Cook for a minute until thick and smooth, then remove the pan from the heat and beat in the 3 egg yolks. Add the cream and stir well. Mash the cheese with a little of the sauce, then add it to the rest of the sauce and stir well, until well blended and smooth, or give it a quick whirl in the food processor.

Chop the hard-boiled eggs and stir into the mixture with the chives. Taste and adjust the seasoning if necessary. Soften the gelatine in the water, then dissolve over low heat. When thoroughly dissolved, gently stir the gelatine into the mousse and leave until half set.

Whisk the egg whites until stiff, fold them into the mousse and turn it into a 1.4-litre/2½-pint mould. Chill thoroughly until firm.

To serve, turn the mousse out on to a plate and add bunches of watercress. If you are taking the mousse on a picnic, then pack it in a mould which has a tight-fitting lid. Keep it on ice until ready to serve it, then turn out and garnish.

BEETROOT ROULADE

SERVES 6

This is light and delicate, and perfect for a warm sunny day. Serve with a large green salad.

175 g/6 oz Emmental cheese
50 g/2 oz fresh breadcrumbs
salt and pepper
100 g/4 oz cooked beetroot
150 ml/¼ pint soured cream
4 eggs, separated
handful of fine dry white breadcrumbs
FILLING
225 g/8 oz cream cheese
4 tablespoons creamed horseradish

Grate the cheese and mix it with the breadcrumbs, then stir in seasoning. Grate the beetroot, add it to the mixture and stir in the soured cream with the egg yolks.

Line a 23 × 33-cm/9 × 13-in Swiss roll tin with non-stick cooking parchment. Grease this thoroughly and sprinkle the base with the dry breadcrumbs. Whisk the egg whites until they stand in stiff peaks, fold into the beetroot mixture and turn it into the tin. Pour it evenly over the surface, then spread out gently, trying not to disturb the crumbs.

Bake the roulade in a moderately hot oven (200 C, 400 F, gas 6) for 10 to 12 minutes, until set. While the roulade is cooking beat the cream cheese and creamed horseradish together. Turn the roulade out on to a sheet of greaseproof paper and remove the cooking parchment. Spread the filling over and roll up, using the greaseproof paper as a guide. Trim off the ends, sprinkle with grated raw beetroot and serve sliced.

NOTE: If the cream cheese mixture seems too thick, add a little cream.

STUFFED POTATO SHELLS

(Illustrated overleaf)

SERVES 6

6 large potatoes
melted butter for brushing
COTTAGE CHEESE FILLING
3 celery sticks
2 large dessert apples
a few spring onions
100 g/4 oz walnuts or salted peanuts
handful of sultanas
freshly grated nutmeg
salt and pepper
350 g/12 oz cottage cheese
CARROT AND RADISH FILLING
225 g/8 oz carrots, grated
juice of 1 lemon
bunch of radishes, thinly sliced
2 tablespoons chopped chives
100 g/4 oz wholemeal breadcrumbs
50 g/2 oz butter
4 tablespoons soured cream
MUSHROOM AND COURGETTE FILLING
225 g/8 oz button mushrooms, sliced
2 courgettes, finely sliced
1 red onion, chopped
2 tablespoons chopped fresh marjoram
150 ml/¼ pint soured cream

Bake the potatoes in their jackets in a moderately hot oven (200 C, 400 F, gas 6) for about an hour or until they are cooked through. Leave them to cool slightly, then cut each one in half and scoop out the middle using a small spoon. Leave a fairly thick skin, then brush the potato shells with melted butter, both inside and out, and place them on a baking tray. Put them back in the oven for a further 20 minutes, or until the shells are really crisp.

For the cottage cheese filling, chop the celery, core and chop the apples and the spring onions. Mix all these ingredients with the walnuts or peanuts, sultanas, a good sprinkling of nutmeg and seasoning, and the cottage cheese.

For the second filling, mix the carrots, lemon juice, radishes and chives and put them in a bowl. Fry the breadcrumbs in the butter until crisp, then turn into the bowl and mix with the cream. Mix all the ingredients for the mushroom and courgette filling.

When the potato skins are cooked, fill them with the mixtures and serve as soon as possible. If you like, leave the skins to cool before filling them but do not fill them too long before you eat them or they will become soggy.

FILLED LYCHEES

SERVES 4

To serve with drinks.

20 canned lychees
50 g/2 oz peanuts, roasted and finely chopped
a little finely chopped fresh root ginger (about 1 teaspoon is enough or the filling will be too hot)
50 g/2 oz Philadelphia cheese

Thoroughly drain and dry the lychees. Beat the nuts and ginger into the cheese, then use a small spoon to press this mixture into the stoned lychees. Chill before serving.

NOTE: If you possess a cherry stoner, stone some cherries and stuff with this mixture.

ASPARAGUS WITH HAM SAUCE

SERVES 4

450 g/1 lb asparagus spears, trimmed
salt and pepper
100 g/4 oz cooked ham, minced
1 tablespoon Dijon mustard
150 ml/¼ pint soured cream
2 tablespoons lemon juice

Tie the asparagus in a neat bundle, then cook it in boiling salted water for about 7 to 10 minutes. Drain and set aside. Mix all the sauce ingredients and chill. Serve with the asparagus.

Above: Stuffed Potato Shells (previous page);
opposite: Green Bean Salad (page 52)

GREEN BEAN SALAD

(Illustrated on previous page)

SERVES 4

450 g / 1 lb young French beans
75 g / 3 oz pine nuts, lightly toasted
6 slices bread
50 g / 2 oz butter
2 tablespoons olive oil
1 clove garlic, crushed
4 eggs, hard-boiled
1 red onion, thinly sliced
1 tablespoon chopped fresh marjoram

DRESSING

4 tablespoons olive oil
2 tablespoons cider vinegar
1 tablespoon clear honey
salt and pepper
2 teaspoons wholegrain mustard

Trim the beans, then steam them for 3 to 5 minutes, so that they are tender but still very crisp. Put the beans in a bowl with the pine nuts.

Cut the crusts off the bread if you like, then cut the slices into small cubes. Melt the butter with the oil in a large pan. When hot add the garlic and the bread cubes. Cook, stirring and turning the cubes frequently, until they are evenly brown and crisp. Discard garlic. Drain on absorbent kitchen paper and add these croûtons to the beans and pine nuts.

Quarter the eggs and separate the onion slices into rings, then add both to the salad. If you are taking this a distance, pack it into a container at this point and take the dressing separately, to be added at the last minute. Sprinkle the marjoram over the top. Put all the dressing ingredients together in a screw-topped jar and shake well, then pour this over the salad. Lightly toss.

CREAMED RICE DESSERT

SERVES 6

65 g / 2½ oz short-grain rice
50 g / 2 oz caster sugar
2 teaspoons vanilla essence
600 ml / 1 pint milk
50 g / 2 oz butter
grated nutmeg
handful of sultanas
4 tablespoons rum
100 g / 4 oz hazelnuts, chopped and toasted
300 ml / ½ pint double cream

Wash the rice, put it in a saucepan with plenty of cold water and bring to the boil. Cook for a minute, drain and put in a greased ovenproof dish. Add the sugar and vanilla, pour on the milk and dot with the butter, add a sprinkling of nutmeg. Put the pudding in a moderate oven (160 C, 325 F, gas 3) for 1½ hours, or until the rice is cooked and the pudding is quite thick. Stir the pudding fairly frequently after the first 45 minutes, to prevent a skin from forming. Soak the sultanas in the rum.

Add the sultanas and rum with the nuts to the hot pudding, then set it aside to cool. When cold, chill thoroughly. Whip the cream and fold it into the rice. Spoon the dessert into wine or champagne glasses.

NOTE: You can stir in sliced banana at the last minute.

BLUEBERRY-FILLED CHEESECAKE

SERVES 6 TO 8

BASE
100 g/4 oz digestive biscuits, crushed
50 g/2 oz hazelnuts, toasted and chopped
50 g/2 oz butter
BLUEBERRY FILLING
450 g/1 lb blueberries plus some whole ones for decoration
25 g/1 oz caster sugar
15 g/$\frac{1}{2}$ oz gelatine
3 tablespoons water
CREAM CHEESE FILLING
225 g/8 oz cream cheese
grated rind and juice of 1 lemon
50 g/2 oz caster sugar
150 ml/$\frac{1}{4}$ pint natural yogurt (use the very creamy thick Greek-type)
3 tablespoons orange liqueur
15 g/$\frac{1}{2}$ oz gelatine
3 tablespoons water
2 egg whites

Mix the crushed biscuits with the nuts. Melt the butter and stir in the biscuit mixture. Press this into the base of an 18-cm/7-in springform tin and chill.

First make the blueberry filling. Put the blueberries in a pan with the sugar and cook gently for just a few minutes until the juice runs then remove from the heat. Dissolve the gelatine in the water over a pan of simmering water, then stir it into the blueberries and leave until almost set.

Beat the cream cheese with the lemon rind and juice, then stir in the sugar and the yogurt. Add the liqueur, stir and set aside. Soften the gelatine in the water then dissolve over low heat. Stir it into the cream cheese mixture and chill until half set. Whisk the egg whites until stiff, then fold them into the mixture.

Put half the cream cheese on top of the biscuit crust, spreading it out evenly. Spoon the half-set blueberry mixture on top, then add the rest of the cream cheese mixture. Smooth the top and chill until completely set.

To remove the cheesecake from the tin, gently run a knife around the inside, then undo the springform sides. Top the cheesecake with whole blueberries, piled up in the middle just before you serve it.

If you don't care about calories, serve the cheesecake with cream flavoured with orange liqueur. After all, tomorrow is another day.

REDCURRANTS WITH YOGURT

SERVES 6

This looks nice served in wine glasses.

450 g / 1 lb redcurrants
600 ml / 1 pint thick creamy natural yogurt
honey to taste
redcurrants on stalks to decorate

String the redcurrants and chill them thoroughly. Make sure that the yogurt is really well chilled.

Stir the honey into the yogurt. Layer the red-currants and yogurt into a glass dish, then decorate with currants on their stalks. The dessert should be served very cold. Looks nice in wine glasses.

NOTE: Equally delicious with blackberries or blackcurrants.

APRICOT TARTS

MAKES 12

SWEET PASTRY
100 g/4 oz plain flour
65 g/2½ oz butter
25 g/1 oz caster sugar
1 egg yolk
CRÈME PÂTISSIÈRE
25 g/1 oz cornflour
25 g/1 oz caster sugar
300 ml/½ pint milk
vanilla pod
2 egg yolks
2 tablespoons double cream
TOPPING
6 ripe apricots
GLAZE
3 tablespoons apricot jam

Sift the flour for the pastry into a bowl, then rub in the butter and stir in the sugar. Add the egg yolk and mix to make a smooth soft pastry. Chill briefly, then roll out thinly and use to line 12 small tart tins. Prick the pastry with a fork and chill the tart cases for 30 minutes before cooking them. Bake in a moderately hot oven (200 C, 400 F, gas 6) for about 15 minutes, or until the pastry is cooked and pale brown. Leave in the tins for a minute or so, then carefully lift the tart cases and transfer them to a wire rack to cool completely.

Blend the cornflour to a smooth paste with the sugar and a little of the milk. Pour the rest of the milk into a saucepan and add the vanilla pod, splitting it to release the flavour. Bring to the boil over a low heat, then leave to stand for 5 minutes before removing the pod. Pour the milk on to the cornflour mixture, stirring all the time, then return to the pan and bring back to the boil, again stirring to prevent the mixture from becoming lumpy. Remove from the heat and beat in first the egg yolks then the cream. Leave to cool.

Peel, halve and stone the apricots. Heat the jam in a small saucepan, sieve if you have time. When the crème pâtissière has cooled divide it between the tart cases and chill until set. Put an apricot half on each tartlet and brush the glaze over the top. Chill lightly before serving.

NOTE: If you can be bothered, crack open the apricot stones and sprinkle the kernels over the tarts, or top with toasted almonds. Use other fruits for this as they come into season.

GREENGAGE DESSERT

SERVES 4 TO 6

This is so simple – but it is a lovely way of using greengages.

450 g/1 lb greengages
3 tablespoons honey
2 tablespoons water
300 ml/½ pint double cream
a few hazelnuts, chopped and toasted

Stone the greengages and place in a saucepan with the honey and water. Cover and cook over a gentle heat until soft. Purée the fruit in a food processor. When cold, whip the cream until thick and fold into the fruit purée. Spoon into individual glasses and sprinkle with the chopped nuts.

NOTE: I also use plums for this.

APPLE AND CHERRY STRUDEL

SERVES 6 TO 8

225 g/8 oz cooking apples
50 g/2 oz caster sugar
300 ml/½ pint water
225 g/8 oz fresh cherries, stoned
50 g/2 oz hazelnuts, chopped and toasted
½ teaspoon ground cinnamon
grated rind of 1 orange
8 sheets philo pastry
50 g/2 oz butter, melted
GLAZE
2 tablespoons apricot jam
1 tablespoon boiling water
icing sugar to sprinkle
50 g/2 oz hazelnuts, chopped and toasted, for topping

Peel, core and slice the apples, put them in a saucepan. Add the sugar and water. Cook for about 20 minutes or until the fruit is soft and thick. Put the mixture in a food processor and blend it briefly to make a rough purée. Stir in the cherries, nuts, cinnamon and orange rind, then leave to cool completely.

Lay a sheet of pastry, doubled over, on the work surface. Spread the filling over it up to 2.5 cm/1 in of the edges. Roll up the pastry to enclose the filling. Lay another sheet of pastry on the surface and brush it with a little melted butter, then lift the roll on to one end and roll it up. Continue rolling the strudel in the remaining philo, brushing each sheet with butter.

Put the roll on a greased baking tray and bake in a moderate oven (180 C, 350 F, gas 4) for about 20 minutes, or until golden. Transfer to a wire rack. Sieve the apricot jam and stir in the boiling water, then brush this over the warm strudel and sift icing sugar over the top. Sprinkle the nuts on the strudel and serve warm.

PASSION CAKE

MAKES A 20-CM/8-IN CAKE

175 g/6 oz butter
175 g/6 oz caster sugar
grated rind of 2 oranges
3 eggs
275 g/10 oz self-raising flour
350 g/12 oz carrots, grated
1 teaspoon ground cinnamon
1 teaspoon grated nutmeg
pinch of ground cloves
225 g/8 oz blanched almonds, chopped
175 g/6 oz sultanas
ICING
225 g/8 oz cream cheese
2 tablespoons frozen concentrated grapefruit juice
1 generous tablespoon icing sugar
freshly grated carrot to decorate

Cream the butter and sugar together until pale and soft. Beat in the orange rind, then gradually add the eggs. Fold in the flour, then the carrots with the spices, nuts and fruit. Do not beat the cake mixture at this stage or it will lose all its light airy texture.

Put the mixture in a greased 20-cm/8-in deep cake tin and bake in a moderate oven (160 C, 325 F, gas 3) for 1½ hours. Cool the cake on a wire rack.

For the icing beat all the ingredients together and smooth it over the cake. Decorate with grated carrot if you like.

Summer
Weekends

CHEATING JELLIED BORTSCH

SERVES 4 TO 6

1 small red onion, finely chopped
350 g/12 oz raw beetroot, finely grated
grated rind and juice of 1 lemon
salt and pepper
2 (411-g/14½-oz) cans consommé
TO SERVE
150 ml/¼ pint soured cream
chopped chives

Simply stir all the ingredients together and chill until set. Fork the jellied mixture, then spoon it into individual bowls or wine glasses to serve.

Spoon soured cream on top of each serving and top with chopped chives.

SEAFOOD PÂTÉ

SERVES 6 TO 8

675 g/1½ lb fresh haddock fillet
50 g/2 oz fresh white breadcrumbs
150 ml/¼ pint double cream
grated rind of 2 limes or small lemons
some chopped fennel
2 eggs, separated
salt and pepper
450 g/1 lb peeled cooked prawns

Skin the fish fillet and remove any bones, then mince or whizz it up in a food processor until smooth. Put the fish in a bowl and stir in the breadcrumbs, cream, lime or lemon rind and fennel. Add the egg yolks and mix well, adding plenty of seasoning. Whisk the whites until they stand in stiff peaks, then fold them in carefully.

Chop the prawns and mix them with seasoning. Grease a 1-kg/2-lb loaf tin and line the base with greaseproof paper; grease this thoroughly. Layer the fish and prawn mixtures in the tin, starting and ending with the fish and creating three layers of each. Stand the pâté in a roasting tin half filled with boiling water. Bake in a moderate oven (180 C, 350 F, gas 4) for 1 hour. Leave to cool, then chill thoroughly before turning out. Serve with mayonnaise flavoured with lime.

SMOKED TROUT WITH GUAVA DRESSING

SERVES 4

4 smoked trout
4 lettuce hearts
4 limes
DRESSING
3 guavas
150 ml/¼ pint mayonnaise
a few spring onions, chopped
4 tablespoons double cream
salt and pepper

Arrange the smoked trout on individual plates, with lettuce hearts and a couple of lime halves on each.

Peel the guavas and halve them, then remove the seeds and stalks. Finely chop the fruit and mix it with the mayonnaise, onions, cream and a little seasoning. Serve this dressing lightly chilled.

SALMON PARCELS

SERVES 4

2 ripe avocado pears
225 g/8 oz Philadelphia cheese
dash of Worcestershire sauce
salt and pepper
juice of 1 lemon
2–3 tablespoons soured cream
225 g/8 oz smoked salmon slices
GARNISH
2 small lemons, halved
sprigs of fennel

Halve the pears and remove the stones. Put the flesh in the food processor with the Philadelphia cheese, Worcestershire sauce, seasoning and lemon juice. Add the soured cream and whizz the ingredients together until smooth.

Use the smoked salmon to line four small ramekins (heart shaped dishes are better than round ones) leaving the ends of the slices overhanging the edges of the dishes. Press the salmon into the dishes to make sure there are no gaps. Sprinkle with lemon juice and freshly ground black pepper, then divide the avocado mixture between the dishes and fold the ends of the salmon over the top. The mixture should be completely encased. Press lightly, cover with cling film and put in the refrigerator for a couple of hours.

Turn out on to a large plate, one per person. Put a lemon half on the side and garnish with small sprigs of fennel. Serve with wholemeal or Granary toast.

BAKED MULLET

SERVES 4

4 small red mullet
juice of 1 lemon
salt and pepper
4 tablespoons chopped chives
100 g/4 oz butter
300 ml/½ pint dry white wine
sprigs of dill to garnish

Ask the fishmonger to clean the mullet for you – he may descale them too but if not then do this by scraping off the scales from the tail end towards head end. Hold the fish in the sink because the scales will fly off everywhere.

Wash and dry the mullet, then sprinkle them inside and out with the lemon juice. Season to taste and sprinkle the chives in the fish. Place each mullet on a piece of foil, dot with some of the butter (you should have at least half the quantity left) and pack tightly. Put the packages on a roasting tin and bake in a moderate oven (180 C, 350 F, gas 4) for about 45 minutes.

Pour the wine into a saucepan and bring to the boil. Add all the cooking juices from each package and put the fish on warmed plates; keep hot. Add the remaining butter to the wine and boil hard until the liquid has reduced to one-third of its original quantity. Taste and add seasoning, then pour over the fish. Garnish with dill and serve.

PRAWNS WITH LIME MAYONNAISE

This is a very easy way of preparing brunch, lunch or a light supper. Flavour some home-made mayonnaise with plenty of lime rind and juice, salt and pepper, chopped parsley and chives, and add a few spoonfuls of double cream. (If you don't make your own mayonnaise, then use the best you can buy.) Pile some halved limes in the middle of a big, flattish dish. Arrange some lettuce hearts and spring onions around them, then put whole cooked Mediterranean prawns all round the edge of the dish. Serve the chilled mayonnaise separately.

PINK MAYONNAISE

SERVES 4

225 g/8 oz fresh tomatoes
300 ml/½ pint mayonnaise
4 tablespoons double cream
generous dash of Worcestershire sauce
1 small clove garlic, crushed (optional)
salt and pepper

Cut the tomatoes into pieces, then purée them in a food processor or liquidiser and press them through a sieve. Stir this purée into the mayonnaise. Whip the cream and fold it in with the Worcestershire sauce and garlic (if used). Add seasoning to taste and chill.

Prawns with Lime Mayonnaise

CHICKEN AND SAGE TERRINE

SERVES 6 TO 8

This is great for weekends because it is made at least a day in advance or it freezes well.

1 large onion
2 large cloves garlic, crushed
50 g / 2 oz butter
several sprigs of fresh sage
675 g / 1½ lb uncooked boneless chicken breast
handful of parsley, chopped
salt and pepper
several sprigs of thyme
grated rind of 1 large lemon
4 tablespoons brandy
1 small egg, beaten
50 g / 2 oz breadcrumbs
4 bay leaves
100 g / 4 oz button mushrooms, thinly sliced

Finely chop the onion, sauté it with the garlic in the butter until soft but not browned. Chop the sage and add to the onion, stir well and transfer to a bowl.

Mince the chicken (or whizz it up in a food processor to chop it very finely) and add to the onion mixture with the parsley, plenty of seasoning, the leaves from the thyme, lemon rind, brandy and egg. Stir in the breadcrumbs.

Grease a 1-kg/2-lb loaf tin, dish or terrine. Line the base with greaseproof paper and grease it well. Arrange the bay leaves in the tin.

Put half the chicken mixture into the tin and press it down lightly. Spoon the mushrooms on top and season to taste. Add the remaining chicken mixture, pressing down well. Cover with cooking foil or greaseproof paper and stand in a roasting tin half filled with boiling water. Cook in a moderate oven (180 C, 350 F, gas 4) for 2 hours.

Weight the cooked terrine down with a double thickness of cooking foil and something heavy (a heavy weight from scales or a brick wrapped in greaseproof paper). When cold, chill overnight, then turn out and remove the greaseproof paper. Serve sliced.

SPECIAL EGG TARTS

MAKES 12

12 small tart shells (page 85)
FILLING
3 eggs
6 tablespoons single cream
salt and pepper
50 g / 2 oz butter
bunch of chives, chopped
100 g / 4 oz smoked salmon pieces, chopped

Make the tart shells according to the recipe instructions.

Beat the eggs with the cream and seasoning. Melt the butter in a small, non-stick saucepan over a fairly low heat. Pour in the eggs and cook, stirring all the time, until they set. Do not overcook them or they will curdle.

Remove the pan from the heat and stir in the chives and the smoked salmon. Put spoonfuls of the mixture into the tart shells and serve warm or cold.

NOTE: Serve as a first course or with drinks.

SATURDAY SUPPER CHICKEN

SERVES 6

1.5-kg/3½-lb chicken, boned (ask your butcher to
do this or see page 141)
STUFFING
1 large onion
50 g/2 oz butter
1 clove garlic
grated rind of 2 oranges
225 g/8 oz tomatoes
2 generous tablespoons chopped tarragon
175 g/6 oz buckwheat
300 ml/½ pint water
salt and pepper
50 g/2 oz fresh wholemeal breadcrumbs
a little orange juice
mayonnaise to serve

Lay the chicken flat on a large oiled roasting tin. Cook the onion in the butter with the garlic, until soft but not browned. Add the orange rind and set aside.

Pour boiling water over the tomatoes and leave them for a minute. Drain and use a sharp knife to slide off the skin. Chop the rest, discarding any bits of core. Stir the tomatoes and tarragon into the onion mixture.

Put the buckwheat in a saucepan with the water and add a little seasoning, then bring to the boil, cover and cook gently until the water has been absorbed – about 10 minutes. Remove from the heat and stir in the onion mixture with plenty of seasoning, the breadcrumbs and enough orange juice to bind the mixture together.

Use the stuffing to fill the chicken and sew it up neatly. Dot with butter and roast in a moderately hot oven (190C, 375F, gas 5) for about 1½ hours. Serve hot, or cold with mayonnaise.

CABBAGE PIE

SERVES 6

about 12 large cabbage leaves
a combination of any of the following vegetables,
amounting to about 3 large cups:
celery, cut into fine sticks
runner beans, sliced and cut in half
leeks, cut into strips
green or red pepper, thinly sliced
courgettes, cut into thin strips
cabbage, thinly sliced
3 eggs
175 ml/6 fl oz milk
100 g/4 oz Cheddar cheese, grated
salt and pepper
some chopped herbs of your choice

Remove the thick stems from large cabbage leaves and cook in boiling water until just tender, drain. Butter a 25-cm/ 10-in shallow ovenproof dish and line it with the leaves, leaving them hanging over the edge of the dish. Steam all the remaining vegetables until *just* tender. Fill the cabbage-lined dish with the vegetables.

Beat the eggs with the milk and add the cheese with seasoning to taste. Stir in the herbs and pour the mixture over the vegetables. Fold the cabbage leaves over the top, adding more leaves if necessary to cover the top.

Bake the pie in a moderately hot oven (190C, 375F, gas 5) for about 30 minutes. Turn out and serve hot or cold.

EASY TOMATO AND BASIL SAUCE

SERVES 4

This is delicious with cold poached lemon sole or plain steamed halibut.

6 tomatoes
a few spring onions
1 tablespoon basil leaves
salt and pepper

Put all the ingredients in a food processor or liquidiser and keep whizzing until the mixture is pale and thick. Chill lightly before serving.

MELON AND MANGO WITH LIME

For a light starter, serve wedges of melon with slices of fresh mango. Sprinkle with lime juice and arrange attractively on a serving plate or on individual plates. Add pieces of fresh lime and chill thoroughly before serving.

Melon and Mango with Lime

SUMMER VEGETABLE LASAGNE

SERVES 4 TO 6

225 g/8 oz lasagne (use the type you prefer –
wholemeal, green or the easy-cook one)
1 cauliflower, cooked
450 g/1 lb carrots
450 g/1 lb spinach
3 large onions
75 g/3 oz butter
bay leaf
1 clove garlic, crushed
225 g/8 oz cream cheese
salt and pepper
handful of fresh parsley, chopped
grated rind of 1 orange
freshly grated nutmeg
SAUCE
25 g/1 oz butter
25 g/1 oz plain flour
450 ml/$\frac{3}{4}$ pint milk
100 g/4 oz matured Cheddar cheese, grated

Cook the lasagne in plenty of boiling salted water for about 15 minutes. Drain and rinse under cold water, then put the pieces to one side, laying them on absorbent kitchen paper.

For the fillings, steam the cauliflower until it is tender – about 10 minutes. Cook the carrots in boiling salted water for about 15 to 20 minutes, then drain thoroughly. Trim and shred the spinach, wash the leaves and shake off some of the water. Cook the spinach in the water which remains in the leaves, allowing about 3 to 5 minutes. Drain thoroughly.

Chop the onions and cook them in the butter with the bay leaf until they are soft. Add the garlic, cook for a further few minutes, then remove the bay leaf. Take off the heat. Purée the cauliflower, then beat in half the cream cheese, seasoning and chopped parsley. Add

about a third of the cooked onion.

Purée the carrots, beat in the remaining cream cheese with the orange rind, seasoning and some more parsley. Stir about half the remaining onion into the carrot purée.

You can purée the spinach or leave the leaves whole – whichever you prefer. However, add seasoning and some nutmeg with the remaining onion and stir well, then set aside.

To make the sauce, melt the butter in a saucepan, add the flour and blend well for a minute before stirring in the milk. Bring to the boil and cook for 3 minutes before adding seasoning to taste and most of the cheese. Stir until the cheese melts, then remove the pan from the heat.

Layer the cooked lasagne with the three different vegetables, keeping each type separate. Pour the sauce over the top and sprinkle with the remaining cheese, then bake in a moderate oven (180 C, 350 F, gas 4) for 30 to 35 minutes, or until golden and bubbling.

SPEEDY PASTA

SERVES 6

450 g/1 lb fresh thin noodles
300 ml/$\frac{1}{2}$ pint double cream
50 g/2 oz Parmesan or Cheddar cheese, grated
100 g/4 oz Gorgonzola cheese, crumbled
100 g/4 oz walnuts, roughly chopped
extra cheese to serve

Cook the pasta in boiling salted water for 3 to 4 minutes. Warm the cream with the cheese over a gentle heat, then add the walnuts. Drain the pasta and put it in a serving dish, then pour the sauce over and serve sprinkled with extra cheese.

TUNA CANNELLONI

SERVES 4

12 cannelloni tubes
50 g/2 oz butter · 50 g/2 oz plain flour
600 ml/1 pint milk · salt and pepper
2 teaspoons dried oregano
some chopped parsley
50 g/2 oz Cheddar cheese, grated
25 g/1 oz Parmesan cheese, grated
150 ml/¼ pint soured cream
2 (198-g/7-oz) cans tuna in brine, drained
a few spring onions, chopped
50 g/2 oz button mushrooms, chopped
juice of 1 lemon
TOPPING
cupful of breadcrumbs
a little extra Parmesan cheese, grated

Cook the cannelloni tubes in plenty of boiling salted water for about 10 minutes, or until they are tender but not too soft. (Or use the type which doesn't need pre-cooking.) Drain thoroughly and rinse under cold water, then set aside on a double-thick piece of absorbent kitchen paper.

Melt the butter in a saucepan. Add the flour, blend well and pour in the milk, still stirring. Bring to the boil, stirring all the time, then add seasoning, the herbs and both lots of cheese. Stir over a low heat until the cheese melts, then remove from the heat and add the cream.

Flake the tuna into a bowl, add the onions and mushrooms with the lemon juice and seasoning. Add about a quarter of the sauce to bind the mixture.

Fill the drained cannelloni with the tuna mixture, then put them in a buttered ovenproof dish and pour the rest of the sauce over the top. Sprinkle with the breadcrumbs and cheese for topping and bake in a moderately hot oven (180 C, 350 F, gas 4) for 30 minutes, or until the top is nicely browned and crisp.

SPINACH CANNELLONI

SERVES 4

12 cannelloni tubes (the type which doesn't need pre-cooking)
STUFFING
50 g/2 oz butter
1 (225-g/8-oz) packet frozen chopped spinach, defrosted and squeezed dry
225 g/8 oz cottage cheese
4 tablespoons double cream
1 egg, beaten
salt and pepper
grated nutmeg
50 g/2 oz Cheddar cheese, grated
SAUCE
50 g/2 oz butter
50 g/2 oz plain flour
600 ml/1 pint milk
75 g/3 oz Cheddar cheese, grated
TOPPING
50 g/2 oz fresh breadcrumbs
50 g/2 oz Cheddar cheese, grated

Mix all the stuffing ingredients together and carefully fill the cannelloni tubes. Lay in a greased ovenproof dish.

For the sauce, melt the butter and stir in the flour. Pour in the milk, bring to the boil and add seasoning. Cook for 2 to 3 minutes and stir in the cheese.

Pour the sauce over the cannelloni and sprinkle with the topping. Bake in a moderate oven (180 C, 350 F, gas 4) until brown and bubbly.

NOTE: For a large group of people make both spinach and tuna cannelloni.

SANDWICH SOUFFLÉ

SERVES 6

This dish is better if you prepare it in advance so that the egg and milk mixture has really soaked into the bread. In actual fact, plain cheese sandwiches are the nicest but here are different fillings.

18 slices bread · 75 g/3 oz butter
225 g/8 oz ricotta cheese
large bunch of mixed fresh herbs, chopped
salt and pepper
175 g/6 oz Cheddar cheese, sliced
100 g/4 oz cooked ham, sliced
175 g/6 oz Wensleydale cheese
1 large red pepper
3 eggs · 300 ml/½ pint milk
extra Cheddar cheese, grated, for topping

Cut the crusts off the bread if you like, then butter the slices. Beat the ricotta with the herbs and seasoning to taste. Sandwich six slices of the bread and butter together with the ricotta and herbs and another six with the Cheddar cheese and ham.

Crumble the white cheese. Cut the top off the pepper, remove the seeds and chop the shell, then mix this with the crumbled cheese. Sandwich the remaining bread and butter together with this mixture. Press all the sandwiches together firmly, cut in half or quarters.

Beat the eggs with the milk and seasoning. Put the sandwiches in a greased ovenproof dish. Pour the egg and milk over the top and leave to soak for at least an hour. Dot with any remaining butter and sprinkle with the grated Cheddar. Bake in a moderately hot oven (190 C, 375 F, gas 5) for about 40 to 45 minutes, until golden and set. Serve at once.

ROSE PETAL AND PISTACHIO ICE CREAM

SERVES 8 TO 10

6 eggs
50 g/2 oz caster sugar
600 ml/1 pint milk
petals from two roses
300 ml/½ pint double cream
100 g/4 oz pistachio nuts, chopped

Separate 4 eggs, then put the yolks in a bowl with the remaining whole eggs and the sugar. Set the whites aside. Beat the eggs and sugar together until pale, then add the milk. Stand the bowl over a saucepan of barely simmering water and cook the mixture (stirring all the time) until it thickens enough to coat the back of a spoon. Do not overheat it or it will curdle. Remove the bowl from the heat and continue to stir until cooled.

Add the rose petals to the custard. Whip the cream until it forms soft peaks, then fold into the custard. Lightly stir in the nuts. Whisk the egg whites until they stand in stiff peaks, then fold them into the mixture and pour it into a freezer container or an ice cream maker. Freeze until icy, then whisk thoroughly and return the ice cream to the freezer. Repeat this process about three times, then leave the ice cream to freeze. If you are using an ice cream maker there is no need to whisk the ice crystals out of the mixture.

To serve, put the ice cream in the refrigerator for 20 to 30 minutes so that it is soft enough to scoop. Use rose petals to decorate individual portions of the ice cream.

QUICK LYCHEE SORBET

SERVES 4

1 (312-g/11-oz) can lychees
4 tablespoons icing sugar
juice of 1 large lemon

Put all the ingredients in a liquidiser or food processor and blend until smooth. Pour into a freezer container and freeze until half frozen, then return the mixture to the liquidiser or food processor and process until smooth. Pour the sorbet back into the container and freeze until hard. Leave in the refrigerator for about 20 minutes before serving.

LAVENDER ICE CREAM

SERVES 6

about 2–3 tablespoons lavender flowers
150 ml/¼ pint milk
pared rind of ½ lemon
4 tablespoons clear honey
300 ml/½ pint double cream

Make sure the lavender is clean and put it in a saucepan with the milk. Add the lemon rind, heat very slowly until the milk boils and leave to cool. Strain the milk, squeezing the lavender to extract all the flavour. Stir in the honey.

Whip the cream until just thick and slowly whisk in the milk. Pour into a freezer container and freeze until firm. Put in the refrigerator for about 20 minutes before serving.

BROWNIES

MAKES 16 PIECES

100 g/4 oz bitter chocolate
150 g/5 oz butter
4 eggs
175 g/6 oz sugar
225 g/8 oz self-raising flour
1 teaspoon vanilla essence
225 g/8 oz walnuts, roughly chopped

Melt the chocolate with the butter in a small saucepan over a low heat. Set aside to cool. Beat the eggs, then beat in the sugar and the cooled chocolate and butter. Stir in the flour, vanilla and nuts.

Grease a 20-cm/8-in square tin, then turn the mixture into it and bake in a moderate oven (180 C, 350 F, gas 4) for 50 to 60 minutes. Leave to cool in the tin and cut into squares when cold.

NOTE: You can serve the brownies warm as an impromptu pudding eaten with double cream whipped with rum and a little icing sugar.

SWEET CARROT TART

SERVES 6 TO 8

225 g/8 oz plain flour
100 g/4 oz butter or margarine
about 3 tablespoons water
FILLING
100 g/4 oz carrots, grated
25 g/1 oz raisins
1 teaspoon grated nutmeg
2 eggs
150 ml/¼ pint double cream
75 g/3 oz wholemeal breadcrumbs
4 tablespoons brandy
grated rind and juice of 1 orange
a little lemon juice

Sift the flour into a bowl and rub in the butter, then stir in the water to bind the ingredients. Roll out the pastry and use to line a 20-cm/8-in loose-bottomed flan tin. Bake blind in a moderate oven (180 C, 350 F, gas 4) for 10 minutes.

Beat all the filling ingredients together, pour into the flan and continue to cook for a further 40 minutes, until lightly golden and firm to the touch. Serve warm or cold.

✿
EXOTIC
FRUIT
BASKET

Have a large flat basket and fill it with all sorts of delicious fruits. Guavas, passion fruit, fresh dates, cherries, nectarines and plums; mounds of blueberries, strawberries, blackberries and raspberries; slices of melon and pineapple; bunches of black and green grapes; bananas, figs, prickly pears and kiwi fruit. Arrange with some leaves and some flowers, and put in the centre of the table.

With some muffins, fresh juice and coffee you have a no-hassle breakfast or brunch for lots of people, also something attractive to look at.

Above: Wholemeal Croissants (page 96) with Instant Jam (page 93); opposite: Exotic Fruit Basket

SIMPLE WEEKEND CAKE

MAKES A 20-CM/8-IN CAKE

This is quick to make and useful if you suddenly find you have extra guests.

275 g/10 oz plain flour
½ teaspoon salt
½ teaspoon bicarbonate of soda
2 teaspoons baking powder
175 g/6 oz light soft brown sugar
grated rind of 1 orange
50 g/2 oz walnuts, chopped
2 ripe bananas, mashed
175 g/6 oz carrots, grated
3 eggs, beaten
175 ml/6 fl oz sunflower oil
SIMPLE FROSTING
175 g/6 oz Philadelphia cheese
2 generous tablespoons frozen concentrated orange juice
2 tablespoons icing sugar
about 6 tablespoons double cream or soured cream

Sift the flour, salt, bicarbonate of soda and baking powder into a bowl. Add the sugar, orange rind, walnuts, bananas and carrots. Mix well, then add the eggs and the sunflower oil and beat for 1 minute.

Line the base of a 20-cm/8-in deep cake tin and grease the tin. Turn the mixture into the tin and bake in a moderate oven (180 C, 350 F, gas 4) for 1 hour 20 minutes. Turn the cake out to cool on a wire rack.

Put the Philadelphia cheese into a bowl, then beat in the remaining ingredients for the frosting. Pile this on top of the cooled cake, or slit the cake horizontally and sandwich it together with frosting if you prefer.

FRESH PEACH CAKE

MAKES A 23-CM/9-IN CAKE

This is one of those useful recipes because you can freeze the cake on a day when you are not very busy and it's a delicious cake to have either with tea or as a dessert.

4 eggs
100 g/4 oz caster sugar
grated rind of 2 lemons
100 g/4 oz plain flour
25 g/1 oz butter, melted
FILLING
6 ripe peaches
300 ml/½ pint double cream
4 tablespoons rum
2 tablespoons icing sugar
8 ratafia biscuits

Beat the eggs and sugar together with the lemon rind until they are very pale and thick. Sift the flour and gently fold it into the eggs. Lastly fold in the melted butter.

Line the base of two 23-cm/9-in sandwich tins with greaseproof paper and grease them thoroughly. Divide the mixture between the tins and bake the cakes in a moderately hot oven (190 C, 375 F, gas 5) for about 25 minutes. Remove the cakes from their tins and leave them to cool on a wire rack.

Put the peaches in a large bowl and pour on enough boiling water to cover them. Leave for a minute, then drain and peel the fruit. Halve the peaches, remove the stones and chop. Put the cream, rum and icing sugar in a bowl, then whip the mixture until firm. Crumble the ratafias and mix them with the chopped peaches. When they are well combined, fold the mixture into the whipped cream.

Sandwich the two sponges together with about two-thirds of the mixture, then spread the rest over the top. Chill well before serving.

FLORENTINES

MAKES ABOUT 18

Marvellous with tea or with coffee instead of a dessert, or with plain vanilla ice cream.

90 g / 3½ oz butter
100 g / 4 oz sugar
150 g / 5 oz mixed nuts (almonds mainly, if possible, mixed with walnuts and hazelnuts)
150 g / 5 oz candied lemon and orange peel, chopped
2 tablespoons double cream

M elt the butter in a saucepan and add the sugar. Stirring all the time, bring slowly to the boil. Remove the pan from the heat and add everything, the cream last. Stir well.

Line baking trays with rice paper, then put teaspoonfuls of mixture well apart on the paper. Bake in a moderate oven (180 C, 350 F, gas 4) for about 10 minutes or until lightly brown. Leave to cool slightly on the tins, then remove the florentines to a wire rack to cool completely.

Trim the edges of the cooled rice paper. You can cover the back of the florentines with melted chocolate or just leave them plain. I leave mine plain.

NOTE: To make an interesting dessert, place florentines all round a serving dish (sticking up). Fill centre with vanilla ice cream.

PORT WINE BISCUITS

MAKES ABOUT 40

100 g / 4 oz butter
100 g / 4 oz caster sugar
2 egg yolks
2 tablespoons port
grated rind of 1 orange
225 g / 8 oz plain flour
¼ teaspoon cinnamon
salt
¼ teaspoon baking powder
100 g / 4 oz ground almonds
100 g / 4 oz blanched almonds, chopped
TO FINISH
port for brushing
caster sugar to sprinkle

C ream the butter with the sugar until soft and pale. Beat in the egg yolks, port and orange rind. Mix in all the remaining ingredients and take pieces of the mixture about the size of walnuts. Roll into balls, then put on greased baking trays and flatten the mixture. Bake in a moderately hot oven (200 C, 400 F, gas 6) for 10 to 12 minutes. Brush with port and sprinkle with caster sugar as soon as the biscuits are removed from the oven, then cool on wire racks.

Lazy Summer Sundays

ICED APRICOT SOUP

SERVES 6

1.5 kg/3 lb apricots
450 ml/¾ pint sweet white wine
1 cinnamon stick
150 ml/¼ pint single cream
about 3–4 tablespoons natural yogurt

Halve the apricots and remove their stones. Put them in a pan with the wine and cinnamon stick. Bring to the boil and simmer gently until the fruit is very soft. Purée, then sieve the soup and leave to cool completely.

Stir in the cream and chill the soup for about an hour. Stir in the yogurt just before serving, or swirl it into each portion if you like.

NOTE: To go with this soup make some miniature muffins. Follow the recipe on page 97 but cook the mixture in very small bun tins and shorten the time so that the muffins do not overcook.

KEDGEREE SPECIAL

SERVES 4

1 large onion, chopped
50 g/2 oz butter
225 g/8 oz long-grain rice
½ teaspoon turmeric
600 ml/1 pint chicken stock
450 g/1 lb peeled cooked shrimps or prawns
some chopped parsley
225 g/8 oz shelled peas
grated rind of 2 lemons
4 hard-boiled eggs, chopped
TO SERVE
4 tablespoons soured cream, warmed
bunch of dill, broken into fine sprigs

Cook the onion in the butter until soft but not browned. Add the rice and the turmeric, cook for a minute and pour in the stock. Bring to the boil, cover the pan and simmer gently for 25 minutes or until the liquid has been absorbed.

Add the shrimps or prawns, parsley and peas, then add the lemon rind and re-cover the pan. Leave over a low heat for a few minutes. Add the eggs and fork all the ingredients together. Transfer the mixture to a hot serving dish. Pour over the warmed cream and sprinkle with the dill.

CRAB AND GRAPEFRUIT

SERVES 8

1 (215-g/7½-oz) packet frozen puff pastry, defrosted
1 egg, beaten
225 g/8 oz cream cheese
4 tablespoons soured cream
¼ teaspoon paprika
4 pink grapefruit
225 g/8 oz crab meat
salt and pepper
SAUCE
2 ripe avocado pears
150 ml/¼ pint soured cream
bunch of chives, chopped
a few drops of lemon juice
GARNISH
sprigs of lemon balm
some Iceberg lettuce, shredded

Roll out the pastry very thinly into an oblong shape measuring about 15 × 50 cm/6 × 20 in, then cut it into four pieces. Prick the pastry all over with a fork, lay the pieces on baking trays and glaze them with some of the beaten egg. Bake in a hot oven (230 C, 450 F, gas 8) for 10 to 12 minutes. Transfer to wire racks to cool.

Beat the cream cheese with the soured cream and paprika. Grate the rind from one of the grapefruit and add to the cream cheese mixture. Cut all the peel and pith off the fruit, then cut between the membranes and remove the segments (if you do this over a bowl you will catch all the juice). Flake the crab meat and mix it with the fruit segments, adding seasoning.

Halve, peel and stone the avocados, then mash them until smooth and add the chives, lemon juice and soured cream. Blend well and chill quickly in the freezer.

Spread the pastry with the cream cheese mixture, then top with the crab meat and grapefruit, and lemon balm. Arrange on a serving dish and surround with the shredded lettuce. Eat topped with the avocado sauce. Follow this with a sorbet and you have a delicious lunch.

STUFFED APPLES

(Illustrated on page 86)

SERVES 4

Useful for a light lunch or as an unusual starter.

2 large smoked mackerel fillets, flaked
2 hard-boiled eggs, chopped
bunch of parsley, chopped
bunch of chives, chopped
salt and pepper
about 3 tablespoons soured cream
1 tablespoon mayonnaise
1 generous tablespoon creamed horseradish
4 large crisp dessert apples
a little lemon juice

Make sure there are no bones or pieces of skin in the flaked mackerel, then mix it with the eggs, herbs and seasoning to taste. Add the soured cream, mayonnaise and horseradish.

Cut the tops off the apples and keep these for lids. Scoop out the apples with a small sharp knife to leave hollow shells and sprinkle the insides with a little lemon juice to prevent them from turning brown. Cut the apple flesh into cubes discarding the cores, then add the fruit to the mackerel mixture. Stir well, use to fill the apples, then replace the lids. Serve soon after the apples are filled.

NOTE: The mackerel and egg mixture can be prepared the evening before, if you like, ready to have the apple mixed in at the last minute.

PICK-ME-UP BREAKFAST

P ut into the liquidiser 300 ml/$\frac{1}{2}$ pint chilled milk, 1 egg, 1 banana (cut up), honey to taste and grated nutmeg. Whirl until frothy, pour into a tall glass and drink slowly. Add a large multi-vitamin tablet and you can forget about eating anything for the rest of the day.

Above: Small Vegetable Tarts (page 85); opposite: Savoury Jelly (overleaf)

SAVOURY JELLY

(*Illustrated on previous page*)

SERVES 6 TO 8

600 ml/1 pint white grape juice
25 g/1 oz gelatine
a few sprigs of mint · 1½ cucumbers
2 tablespoons white wine vinegar
225 g/8 oz seedless white grapes
salt and pepper

Use about 6 tablespoons of the grape juice to dissolve the gelatine over a low heat.

Roughly chop the mint and add it to the remaining grape juice and the dissolved gelatine. Peel and coarsely grate the cucumbers, squeeze out all the excess liquid, add the vinegar and stir then add to the grape juice. Halve or quarter the grapes if they are large, add to the mixture. Add seasoning to taste and pour into a 1.4-litre/2½-pint mould. Chill until set.

BAKED AUBERGINE SLICES

SERVES 4

2 large aubergines · salt and pepper
175 g/6 oz fresh wholemeal breadcrumbs
75 g/3 oz Emmental or Cheddar cheese, grated
6–8 tablespoons mayonnaise

Trim the ends off the aubergines, then slice them lengthways. If you have time salt the slices and put in a sieve to drain. Then rinse and pat dry.

Mix the breadcrumbs with the cheese and put the mixture in a thick layer on a plate. Spread both sides of the aubergine slices with mayonnaise, then press into the cheese and breadcrumb mixture so that both sides are thickly coated. Place on a greased baking tray. Bake in a moderately hot oven (200 C, 400 F, gas 6) for 25 to 30 minutes, or until brown and crisp. Sprinkle with chopped parsley. Serve hot as a first course, or for lunch with a salad.

MACKEREL POTS

SERVES 4

50 g/2 oz butter
handful of oatflakes
grated rind of 1 lemon
4 smoked mackerel fillets
4 tablespoons mayonnaise
juice of 1 lemon
4 hard-boiled eggs, chopped
salt and pepper
lemon balm sprigs to garnish

Melt the butter in a pan, then add the oatflakes and cook over a low heat, stirring frequently until lightly browned. Stir in the lemon rind and remove the pan from the heat.

Skin and flake the mackerel, then add it to the oatflakes with the mayonnaise and lemon juice. Stir in the eggs and plenty of seasoning, then put the mixture into individual ovenproof pots or dishes and bake in a moderately hot oven (200 C, 400 F, gas 6) for 8 to 10 minutes. Serve with hot wholemeal toast.

SMALL VEGETABLE TARTS

(Illustrated on page 83)

MAKES 12

Select the freshest, best quality vegetables for these tarts – you won't need large quantities but have a good mixture. Flavour the mayonnaise with lots of chopped herbs, if you like.

50 g/2 oz butter, softened
100 g/4 oz cream cheese
100 g/4 oz self-raising flour
salt and pepper
thinly sliced carrot, tiny cauliflower florets, thinly sliced courgettes, short lengths of French bean
150 ml/¼ pint mayonnaise
1–2 cloves garlic, crushed (optional)

Beat the butter with the cream cheese, then gradually work in the flour and a pinch of salt to make a soft dough. On a lightly floured surface, gently knead the dough into a ball and roll it out thinly. Cut out 12 circles to line patty tins. Press the pastry into the tins, prick all over and chill for 30 minutes.

For the filling the vegetables should be barely cooked. They are best cooked separately by steaming and 3 to 5 minutes is quite long enough. Leave them to cool.

Bake the tartlet cases in a moderately hot oven (200 C, 400 F, gas 6) for 10 to 15 minutes or until the pastry is crisp and golden. Leave the tarts in the tins for a few minutes, then transfer them to a wire rack to cool.

Pile the vegetables (separately or mixed) in the pastry cases. Season the mayonnaise and mix it with the garlic (if you like), then top each of the tarts with some mayonnaise.

Other Vegetables to Try
Asparagus tips, broccoli, tiny peas cooked with shredded lettuce or baby broad beans.

MOULDED SWEET AND SOUR RICE

SERVES 4 to 6

225 g/8 oz brown (or white) long-grain rice
900 ml/1½ pints water
100 g/4 oz nuts, chopped (walnuts, peanuts, Brazils or pine nuts)
50 g/2 oz dried apricots, chopped
handful of sultanas
1 yellow pepper, deseeded and chopped
1 red pepper, deseeded and chopped
a few radishes, thinly sliced
bunch of spring onions, chopped
100 g/4 oz sweet corn
plenty of chopped herbs (parsley, chives, tarragon or basil, all taste good)
salt and pepper
DRESSING
4 tablespoons sunflower oil
1 tablespoon cider vinegar
squeeze of lemon juice
salt and pepper
1 teaspoon honey
large pinch of mustard powder

Put the rice and water in a saucepan, boil and cook until the rice is just tender. Drain well. Add all the remaining ingredients.

Shake all the ingredients for the dressing in a screw-top jar. Stir in the dressing while the rice is still warm. Press into a 1.4-litre/2½-pint ring mould or basin. Leave overnight or for a few hours. Turn out on to a large flat dish. Decorate with watercress, Iceberg lettuce or alfalfa sprouts (or all of these). Sprinkle with a little salad dressing.

Serve this with any cold meats or chicken or ham. Add a large green salad and you have an easy (prepared ahead) minimum-time-in-the-kitchen lunch.

LAZY BREAKFAST OR BRUNCH

A nice way of presenting a late Sunday breakfast (or brunch) is to take a long, flattish basket, line it with leaves (Virginia creeper is always useful for this) and make small piles of different things – rather like an artist's palette – on it. Heap up piles of dried bananas, apricots. Add bunches of black and green grapes, some fresh figs and nectarines, strings of redcurrants and blackcurrants. Add some shelled nuts and flowers.

Put in the middle of the table, with some cheese (what about your Unusual Cheese?), some Ginger Thins or muffins and a large pot of coffee and orange juice.

Above: Stuffed Apples (page 81); opposite: Lazy Breakfast or Brunch

BANANA AND GRAPEFRUIT BUTTER

MAKES ABOUT 450 G / I LB

100 g/4 oz butter · 50 g/2 oz set honey
1 ripe banana, mashed
1 tablespoon frozen concentrated grapefruit juice

Beat the butter and honey together, then beat in the banana and the grapefruit juice. Put into a dish and chill.

UNUSUAL CHEESE

Use all your leftover bits of cheese for this. You will need about 350–450 g/ 12–16 oz of leftover bits plus 175 g/ 6 oz cream cheese.

Place the cheese and cream cheese in a food processor and whizz them round until well blended. If the mixture is too thick add a dash of cream. Scoop the mixture out on to a large piece of cling film then make it into a round shape by completely covering in the cling film and rolling it around.

You can unwrap and cover the cheese in chopped walnuts or chopped herbs if you wish. Then wrap again and keep it refrigerated until you are ready to serve the cheese.

Each time you make this it will taste different, depending on your leftover cheese.

SWEET APPLE OMELETTE

SERVES 4

This makes a refreshingly light breakfast or brunch, or it can be served as a pudding. If you are having it as a pudding, then serve with soured cream.

5 eggs
4 tablespoons single cream
50 g/2 oz caster sugar
grated rind of 1 lemon
½ teaspoon ground cinnamon
2 tablespoons rum
3–4 tart dessert apples
25 g/1 oz butter
a couple of handfuls of sultanas
1 tablespoon brown sugar

Beat the eggs with the cream, sugar, lemon rind, cinnamon and rum. Peel and core the apples, then slice them into rings. Cook these briefly in the butter in a large omelette pan, turning the slices once and adding the sultanas as soon as they are turned.

Beat the egg mixture thoroughly, pour it into the pan on top of the apples and cook over a moderate heat until it is well set underneath, lifting the edges of the mixture to allow unset egg to run into the pan. Have ready a very hot grill. Sprinkle the omelette with brown sugar, put the pan under the grill and finish cooking the top of the omelette until set and golden.

Serve the omelette freshly cooked, cut into wedges.

MELON JELLY

SERVES 4

1 honeydew melon
juice of 1 lemon
75 g/3 oz caster sugar
25 g/1 oz gelatine
4 tablespoons water
150 ml/¼ pint apple juice
fresh mint sprigs, finely chopped

Halve the melon, remove the seeds, then scoop out the flesh and place it in a liquidiser or food processor with the lemon juice and caster sugar. Purée until smooth.

Soften the gelatine in the water then dissolve over gentle heat. Add this to the apple juice, then pour it into the purée and whisk in the mint.

Pour into a 1.4-litre/2½-pint mould and chill until set. Turn the jelly out and serve decorated with lots of mint sprigs.

Alternatively, the mixture can be frozen until slushy, then whisked until smooth and re-frozen until firm to make a melon sorbet. If you do this, then omit the gelatine.

NOTE: You can also return the jelly to the melon skins, then when set, cut into slices and serve.

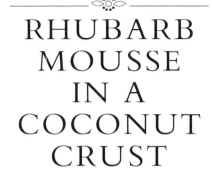

RHUBARB MOUSSE IN A COCONUT CRUST

SERVES 6

450 g/1 lb rhubarb
150 ml/¼ pint plus 4 tablespoons water
50 g/2 oz sugar
50 g/2 oz butter
75 g/3 oz flaked coconut
25 g/1 oz gelatine
300 ml/½ pint double cream

Trim and slice the rhubarb, then put it in a pan with the 150 ml/¼ pint water and the sugar. Bring to the boil, then reduce the heat and cook gently until the rhubarb is tender – about 5 to 10 minutes. Blend the fruit in a food processor or liquidiser.

Melt the butter in a saucepan and add the coconut, cook for a few minutes over a low heat to let it brown slightly. Press into a 23-cm/9-in shallow dish and leave to set in the refrigerator.

Soften the gelatine in the 4 tablespoons water then dissolve over low heat. Stir into the rhubarb and leave until half set. Lightly whip the cream and fold it into the fruit, then pile it into the coconut crust. Chill until firm.

FRESH BLACKBERRIES WITH ORANGE

Fresh fruit in season, simply served, is the perfect answer for the busy cook. For instance don't always use your blackberries for pies – instead put them in a bowl, squeeze the juice from a fresh orange on to them and leave them overnight in the refrigerator. Serve them as they are, or with fresh plain yogurt and honey. Add some home-made muffins and you have a tempting breakfast, brunch or snack.

SUNDAY BISCUITS

MAKES ABOUT 20

These can be made in a flash – useful when the sun is shining and you feel lazy.

100 g/4 oz butter, softened
100 g/4 oz demerara sugar
100 g/4 oz flaked coconut
100 g/4 oz ground rice
50 g/2 oz cornflour
about 4 tablespoons milk

Mix all the ingredients together, adding enough milk to make a soft consistency. Put little mounds of the mixture well apart on greased baking trays and bake in a moderate oven (180 C, 350 F, gas 4) for about 15 minutes or until brown and crisp. Leave to cool slightly on the tins, then transfer to wire racks to cool completely.

Fresh Blackberries with Orange

USEFUL PANCAKES

MAKES ABOUT 24 PANCAKES

225 g/8 oz plain flour (or you can use
wholemeal flour or half-and-half wholemeal and
buckwheat flours)
2 large eggs
generous pinch of salt
600 ml/1 pint milk
butter or oil, or a mixture of both, for cooking

Sift the flour into a bowl. Make a well in the middle and crack in the eggs. Add the salt and some of the milk, then beat well, gradually incorporating the flour and adding more milk to make a smooth batter. Continue beating for a few minutes, then leave the batter, covered, to stand for at least 30 minutes.

To cook pancakes, heat a heavy frying pan and grease it with a little butter or oil. Pour a spoonful of batter on to the pan and tilt it so that the mixture runs all over the surface. Cook until the pancake is golden underneath, then turn it over (or toss it if you are brave, or very competent, or both) and cook on the other side until golden. Continue cooking the pancakes in this way, layering them with pieces of absorbent kitchen paper or greaseproof paper to stop them from sticking together. Add a little water to the batter to keep it thin – if the batter is too thick the pancakes will be heavy. The pancakes can be served hot, but they are also good cold, with different fillings.

Pancake Ideas
Serve the pancakes hot or cold in any of the following ways.

WITH RUM BANANAS: Quickly fry some sliced bananas in butter, add demerara sugar and rum and stir over high heat for a minute. Serve with hot pancakes and whipped cream.

WITH MOCK CAVIAR: Serve bowls of soured cream and chives and red or black mock caviar with the cold pancakes. For these, use batter made with a buckwheat flour mixture.

WITH SLICED MANGO: Fill with sliced mango, fold over and sprinkle with brown sugar. Put under the grill briefly.

BANANA CAKE

MAKES A 1-KG/2-LB LOAF CAKE

225 g/8 oz caster sugar
4 tablespoons sunflower oil
25 g/1 oz butter
2 eggs
3 large ripe bananas, mashed
225 g/8 oz plain flour
¼ teaspoon salt
½ teaspoon ground cinnamon
½ teaspoon ground cloves
75 g/3 oz walnuts, roughly chopped
25 g/1 oz sultanas

Put the sugar in a bowl with the oil and butter, then beat well to cream the mixture. Beat in the eggs, then the bananas.

Sift the flour with the salt and spices. Stir the nuts and sultanas into the flour mixture, then fold this into the banana mixture.

Grease a 1-kg/2-lb loaf tin and turn the mixture into it. Bake in a moderate oven (180 C, 350 F, gas 4) for 1 hour 20 minutes. After an hour, cover the cake with foil to prevent the crust from overbrowning.

Turn the cake out to cool on a wire rack. Serve sliced. You can spread this with mashed banana and honey.

GINGER THINS

MAKES ABOUT 20

225 g/8 oz plain flour
1 teaspoon ground ginger
½ teaspoon ground cinnamon
50 g/2 oz butter
50 g/2 oz soft dark brown sugar
4 tablespoons golden syrup
1 small egg, beaten

Sift the flour, ginger and cinnamon into a bowl. Melt the butter with the sugar and the syrup. Make a well in the dry ingredients, add the melted mixture then the egg, mix together to make a dough.

Turn the dough out on to a floured work surface, knead lightly and roll out very thinly. Cut out round biscuits (about 7.5-cm/3-in circles are best). Put the biscuits on greased baking trays and bake in a moderately hot oven (190 C, 375 F, gas 5) for about 12 minutes. Leave on the trays for a minute, then transfer to wire racks to cool completely.

INSTANT JAM

(*Illustrated on page 74*)

Take advantage of all the fruit in season and before going to bed mash either peaches, raspberries, strawberries or blackberries with a little icing sugar. Put in pots and cover with cling film. Leave in the refrigerator overnight and serve with muffins or croissants for breakfast.

COURGETTE BREAD

MAKES A 1-KG/2-LB LOAF

For breakfast serve warmed bread, thickly sliced, with a selection of marmalades or jams. The courgette bread freezes well and it can be defrosted quickly in either the microwave oven or in the conventional oven.

225 g/8 oz plain flour (or half plain, half wholemeal)
1½ teaspoons baking powder
½ teaspoon bicarbonate of soda
1 teaspoon salt
100 g/4 oz butter
225 g/8 oz courgettes, coarsely grated
50 g/2 oz sunflower seeds
grated rind and juice of 1 orange
2 eggs, lightly beaten
small handful of sunflower seeds to sprinkle on top

Put the flour, baking powder, bicarbonate of soda and salt in a bowl then rub in the butter until the mixture looks like fine breadcrumbs. Stir in the courgettes and sunflower seeds. Add the orange rind and juice, stir then add the eggs. Mix well to combine all the ingredients.

Thoroughly grease a 1-kg/2-lb loaf tin and put the mixture in it. Smooth the top slightly, sprinkle with some sunflower seeds and bake in a moderate oven (180 C, 350 F, gas 4) for about 1½ hours, until well risen and golden on top. Cool the bread on a wire rack.

PLUM ICE CREAM

SERVES 6

This is a really easy ice cream recipe that doesn't need constant attention as it freezes. But still gives a smooth result.

1 kg/2 lb plums, stoned
175 g/6 oz sugar
300 ml/½ pint double cream
50 g/2 oz icing sugar
1 egg yolk
4 tablespoons Kirsch or brandy

Put the plums in a saucepan with any juice you have saved from stoning them. Add the sugar and cook gently, stirring occasionally, until the sugar melts. Poach the fruit for 5 minutes then purée it in a liquidiser or food processor. Leave to cool.

Whip the cream with the icing sugar, egg yolk and Kirsch or brandy until thick, then fold in the cooled fruit purée. Pour the ice cream mixture into a freezer container and freeze for several hours or overnight until firm. Leave the ice cream in the refrigerator for 5 to 15 minutes before scooping it out of the container.

ICED COFFEE

Make some strong black coffee and leave to cool. (Make coffee with 1 teaspoon ground cinnamon added if you like.) Add a dash of brandy and a little single cream, whizz it in a liquidiser. Chill.

Plum Ice Cream in an ice bowl (page 157)

WHOLEMEAL CROISSANTS

(Illustrated on page 74)

MAKES 16

Home-made croissants taste wonderful and they are not too difficult to prepare if you allow enough time for the dough to chill between rolling out the layers. Make a couple of batches when you are in the mood and put the croissants in the freezer. Warm them in a hot oven straight from frozen so that they are crisp.

450 g/1 lb wholemeal flour
1 teaspoon salt
1 teaspoon sugar
400 g/14 oz butter
handful of kibbled wheat plus extra for topping
the croissants
1 (15-g/½-oz) sachet easy-blend yeast
300 ml/½ pint lukewarm water

Put the flour, salt and sugar in a bowl. Add 50 g/2 oz of the butter and rub it in until the mixture is very fine. Cut or shape the remaining butter into four oblong pieces each about the same size as a 225-g/8-oz block but only half the thickness, then chill these thoroughly.

Stir the kibbled wheat and yeast into the flour then add the water and mix the ingredients together to make a dough. Turn the dough out on to the floured surface and knead it thoroughly for 10 minutes until smooth and elastic. Alternatively knead the dough in a food mixer or food processor.

On a well-floured surface shape the dough into an oblong, then roll it out so that it is almost three times longer than it is wide – about 15 × 38–45 cm/6 × 15–18 in. Put one piece of butter in the middle of the dough, fold the bottom third over it then fold the top third down over that. Press the edges together well to seal in the butter then turn the dough so that the short side is nearest you and roll it out to an oblong shape the same size as the original one.

Add the second and third portions of butter, folding and rolling the dough in exactly the same way. Chill it for 10 minutes in the freezer between each rolling if the butter becomes too warm and makes the dough greasy to handle. If the outside of the dough breaks slightly, then keep it well chilled and keep the work surface well floured. Once all the butter is rolled in repeat the folding and rolling process three more times. The more the dough is folded and rolled, the lighter and flakier it will be.

Cut the dough into quarters, keep three pieces chilled as you roll out the fourth into a 30-cm/12-in square. Cut the square diagonally into four triangles. Roll each of these from the longest side towards the point. Put them on a greased baking tray, curving the dough to give the traditional croissant shape. Repeat with the remaining dough to make 16 croissants in all.

Cover the croissants with oiled cling film and leave them in a warm place for 30 to 40 minutes or until they are risen. A grill compartment over the oven is ideal or a warm room will do but do not leave them in a very hot place or the butter will melt and the dough will become very greasy.

Brush the croissants lightly with a little milk and sprinkle them with kibbled wheat then bake them in a hot oven (220 C, 425 F, gas 7) for 12 to 15 minutes or until risen, crisp and brown. Cool on a wire rack.

The croissants taste delicious when served freshly baked and just warm, otherwise put them in an airtight container or sealed polythene bag when completely cold and store them for one or two days. They will still taste great if they are heated through in a hot oven just before serving.

Ideas for Different Croissants
You can make all sorts of croissants by sprinkling fillings, both savoury and sweet, over the triangles of dough before they are rolled up and put to rise. Try some of these suggestions or use your imagination and experiment with some of your own favourite ingredients – nuts, chopped dried fruits, lemon or orange rind, crystallised fruits, grated chocolate and poppy seeds are all suitable.

SESAME AND CHIVES: Sprinkle the triangles of dough with sesame seeds and chopped chives before rolling up. Good with cream cheese.

SPRING ONION AND PARMESAN: Sprinkle the triangles of dough with lots of chopped spring onions and grated Parmesan cheese, then roll up and sprinkle the outside of the croissants with a little extra Parmesan.

HERBS AND NUTS: Sprinkle lots of chopped fresh herbs and chopped mixed nuts over the triangles of dough. Add some raisins and a little grated carrot too, if you like. Serve these croissants with a bowl of cottage cheese mixed with some chopped fresh fruit – peaches, apples, pears or berries.

WALNUT AND ORANGE: Mix some chopped walnuts with grated orange rind and demerara sugar, then sprinkle handfuls over the croissants before rolling them up.

WEEKEND MUFFINS

MAKES 12

250 g/9 oz wholemeal flour (or a mixture of flours)
100 g/4 oz crunchy breakfast cereal or Grape-Nuts
100 g/4 oz brown sugar
3 teaspoons baking powder
¼ teaspoon salt
1 egg, lightly beaten
300 ml/½ pint milk
75 ml/3 fl oz sunflower oil

Stir together the flour, cereal, sugar, baking powder and salt. In another bowl combine the egg, milk and oil, then pour this liquid into the dry ingredients and mix both together. Add any (one or more) of the ingredients given below, if you like. Grease 12 muffin tins and divide the mixture between them, then bake in a moderately hot oven (200 C, 400 F, gas 6) for 20 to 25 minutes.

Ideas for Adding to Muffins
One chopped banana, handful of blueberries, handful of sultanas, chopped nuts and chopped peach.

A GREAT BREAD WITHOUT YEAST

MAKES A MEDIUM LOAF

450 g/1 lb wholemeal flour
a couple of handfuls of kibbled wheat
1 teaspoon salt
25 g/1 oz butter
2 teaspoons bicarbonate of soda
2 teaspoons cream of tartar
100 g/4 oz mixed nuts, finely chopped
400 ml/14 fl oz soured cream (or buttermilk if you prefer)

Put the flour in a bowl with the wheat and salt. Rub in the butter, then add the bicarbonate of soda and the cream of tartar. Stir in the nuts and soured cream to make a soft dough.

Knead the dough lightly, shape it into a round and flatten it slightly on a greased baking tray. Cut a deep cross in the top and bake the bread in a moderately hot oven (200 C, 400 F, gas 6) for 30 minutes. Cool the loaf on a wire rack.

NOTE: This bread freezes well, so make a few loaves when you have the time. Use other sorts of nuts and seeds or grains in the dough to make the loaves different.

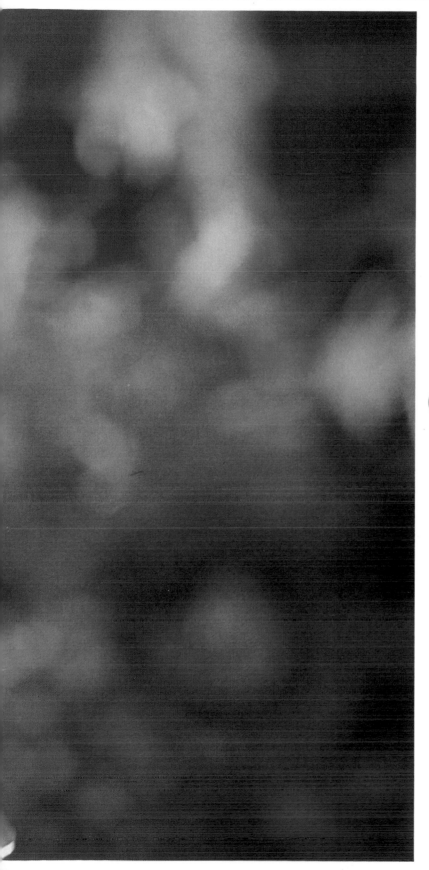

Dinner
Parties

MENU 1

(TO SERVE 4)

Souffléed Tomatoes
or
Cherry Tomato Salad

◇

Poached Turbot Steaks
Minted New Potatoes
Fresh Garden Vegetables

◇

Fresh Figs with Goat's
Cheese
Poppy Seed Straws

I love all vegetables and personally I think they are never more delicious than when they are steamed until just tender (but still crunchy) and left well alone, with perhaps a squeeze of lemon and a grind of pepper. However in this book I have included some recipes for people who like to have something different

SOUFFLÉED TOMATOES

4 beefsteak tomatoes
25 g / 1 oz butter
20 g / $\frac{3}{4}$ oz plain flour
150 ml / $\frac{1}{4}$ pint milk
75 g / 3 oz Parmesan cheese, grated (it's best to use freshly grated if possible)
1 tablespoon basil leaves, chopped
salt · pinch of cayenne
3 eggs, separated
a few dried breadcrumbs

Cut a slice off the top of each tomato, then scoop out the seeds and turn upside down to drain while you make the soufflé mixture.

Melt the butter in a saucepan, stir in the flour and cook for a minute, then gradually add the milk, stirring all the time. Bring to the boil and cook for a minute – the sauce should be very thick. Beat in the cheese and basil, adding seasoning and cayenne to taste. Remove from the heat, add the egg yolks, beat well and set aside to cool slightly.

Blot the insides of the tomatoes with absorbent kitchen paper. Put a few breadcrumbs inside each tomato shell and roll them round tipping out any excess. Whisk the egg whites until they stand in stiff peaks, then stir a spoonful into the sauce. Carefully fold in the rest of the egg whites, divide the mixture between the tomato shells and bake in a hot oven (230 C, 450 F, gas 8) for 10 to 15 minutes, or until risen and brown. Serve immediately.

POACHED TURBOT STEAKS

4 turbot steaks
1 carrot, quartered
1 onion, quartered
bay leaf
bunch of parsley (tied securely)
salt and pepper
150 ml/¼ pint dry white wine
300 ml/½ pint water
GOOSEBERRY SAUCE
450 g/1 lb gooseberries
150 ml/¼ pint water
pared rind of 1 lemon, cut into fine strips
50 g/2 oz sugar
2 tablespoons cider vinegar
2 tablespoons chopped fresh dill
2 spring onions, chopped
GARNISH
dill sprigs · mayonnaise
coarsely grated lemon rind

Rinse and dry the fish steaks. Put all the remaining ingredients for cooking the fish in a large frying pan (a fairly deep one which has a lid) or a large flameproof casserole. If you have a fish kettle, then use that. Bring to the boil, then reduce the heat so that the liquid simmers and put the fish steaks in the pan. Cover and simmer gently for 10 minutes. Remove the pan from the heat and leave the fish to cool completely in the cooking liquid.

Top and tail the gooseberries, then put them in a pan with the water and lemon rind. Add the sugar and cider vinegar, bring to the boil. Reduce the heat and simmer for 10 minutes. Remove from the heat and add the remaining ingredients, leave to cool.

Lift the turbot out of the court bouillon, then remove the skin. Arrange the steaks on a serving dish. Top each fish steak with a little mayonnaise and grated lemon rind. Garnish with dill. Serve the sauce separately.

CHERRY TOMATO SALAD

675 g/1½ lb cherry tomatoes
some basil
6 tablespoons olive oil
juice of 1 lemon
salt and pepper
1 small onion, finely chopped
1 teaspoon sugar
1 teaspoon mustard powder
lettuce leaves to serve

Put the tomatoes in a bowl and cover with boiling water, then drain and peel them. Put the whole tomatoes in a bowl with the leaves from the basil. Put all the rest of the ingredients in a screw-topped jar and shake well. Pour this over the tomatoes and mix thoroughly. Chill before serving on lettuce leaves.

FRESH FIGS WITH GOAT'S CHEESE

Buy several different types of goat's cheese (or other creamy cheeses) and some fresh figs. Arrange the cheeses and halved figs on a large dish or wooden board and serve them with Poppy Seed Straws.

POPPY SEED STRAWS

50 g/2 oz rice flour
175 g/6 oz plain flour
100 g/4 oz butter
75 g/3 oz Cheddar cheese, finely grated
1 tablespoon poppy seeds
1 egg yolk

Mix the flours in a bowl, then rub in the butter and stir in the cheese and poppy seeds. Add the egg yolk to bind the mixture into a firm dough. Roll out on a lightly floured surface into a thin rectangle about 15 cm/6 in wide. Cut into strips (about 1 cm/½ in wide).

Grease one or several baking trays. Twist the strips of biscuit dough and place them on the trays, then bake in a moderately hot oven (200 C, 400 F, gas 6) for 12 to 15 minutes. Cool on wire racks.

MENU 2

(TO SERVE 4)

Fresh Raspberry Soup
(see page 106)

◇

Ratatouille Quiche
Minted Wheat Salad
Green Salad

◇

Grand Marnier Sorbet in
Chocolate Cups

RATATOUILLE QUICHE

225 g/8 oz plain flour
salt and pepper
100 g/4 oz butter or sunflower margarine
50 g/2 oz Parmesan cheese, grated
about 3 tablespoons water
1 large aubergine
1 red pepper
1 green pepper
3 tablespoons olive oil
2 onions, sliced
2 cloves garlic, crushed
350 g/12 oz courgettes, sliced
1 (400-g/14-oz) can chopped tomatoes
2 bay leaves
few leaves of basil, chopped
1 teaspoon oregano
225 g/8 oz mozzarella cheese, sliced

Put the flour in a bowl and add a generous pinch of salt, rub in the butter or margarine until the mixture resembles fine breadcrumbs. Stir in the Parmesan and only just enough of the water to make the pastry bind together. Alternatively, if you have a food processor mix all the ingredients together in that adding water a teaspoonful at a time.

Roll out the pastry on a lightly floured board and use to line a 30 × 20-cm/12 × 8-in loose-bottomed quiche tin. Prick the base all over with a fork and line with a sheet of greaseproof paper. Sprinkle in some dried peas or beans and bake the pastry case in a moderately hot oven (200 C, 400 F, gas 6) for 15 minutes. Remove the paper and beans, then return to the oven for a further 10 minutes.

To make the filling, cut the stalk end and base from the aubergine, then chop the flesh. Place in a colander and sprinkle with salt. Leave on a draining board for 30 minutes. Cut the stalk ends off the peppers, remove any seeds and pith, then slice.

Heat the oil in a heavy-based frying pan — add sliced onions and garlic, and cook until soft but not browned. Remove, set aside. Dry the aubergine with absorbent kitchen paper, cook in oil for a few minutes then remove on to kitchen paper. Now repeat this process with the peppers. Remove. Wipe out pan. Return all the vegetables, plus courgettes and drained, canned tomatoes and herbs. Stir, add a little of the tomato juice. Simmer for 20 minutes covered, then uncover for 10 minutes. Check seasoning, the vegetables should be tender not mushy.

Spoon the filling into the pastry base and cover with the slices of mozzarella. Place the quiche on a flameproof plate and cook under a preheated grill until brown and bubbly. This can also be served cold.

MINTED WHEAT SALAD

(Illustrated on page 134)

225 g/8 oz bulgur
bunch of spring onions
handful of raisins
50 g/2 oz pumpkin seeds, roasted
few sprigs of mint, chopped
grated rind and juice of 1 small lemon
1 clove garlic, crushed
6 tablespoons olive oil or sunflower oil
salt and pepper
lettuce hearts to serve (optional)

Soak the bulgur in cold water for about 30 minutes, then drain it thoroughly and put the grains in a bowl. Chop the spring onions and add them to the bulgur with the raisins, pumpkin seeds and mint.

In a screw-topped jar mix the lemon rind and juice, garlic, oil and plenty of seasoning. Shake well, then pour this dressing over the salad and toss. Marinate for at least 30 minutes. Arrange on lettuce leaves.

GRAND MARNIER SORBET IN CHOCOLATE CUPS

(Illustrated overleaf)

225 g/8 oz plain chocolate
SORBET
225 g/8 oz sugar
900 ml/1½ pints water
grated rind and juice of 2 oranges
6 tablespoons Grand Marnier
1 egg white

Melt the chocolate in a bowl over a saucepan of gently simmering water. Have ready 8 paper cake cases, doubled up to make 4 extra thick ones. Coat the insides of these completely in chocolate, building up the coating as the chocolate sets. Leave in a cool place until the chocolate is hard.

Dissolve the sugar in the water over low heat, then add the orange rind and juice and leave to cool. Stir in the Grand Marnier. Pour the syrup into a container and freeze until ice crystals are forming. Put the mixture into the food processor and whizz it round until the ice is broken down. Whisk the egg white until stiff, fold into the sorbet. Put back in the freezer until it is half frozen, then repeat the process twice to give a smooth sorbet without any ice crystals. If you have an ice cream making machine, freeze the sorbet in that. Once it is smooth, leave in the freezer for several hours or until hard.

To serve, remove the paper cases from around the chocolate cups and place them on individual plates. Leave the sorbet in the refrigerator for about 15 to 20 minutes before serving, so that it is soft enough to scoop. Use a small melon ball scoop and put a few sorbet balls into each chocolate cup.

FRESH RASPBERRY SOUP

1 kg/2 lb raspberries
2 tablespoons icing sugar
300 ml/½ pint Sauternes
300 ml/½ pint single cream

Purée the raspberries in a liquidiser or food processor, then press them through a sieve to remove the seeds. Sweeten the fruit purée with the icing sugar and stir in the wine with about two-thirds of the cream. Chill the soup really well before serving it. It should be *very* cold. Swirl the remaining cream on top.

Above: Grand Marnier Sorbet in Chocolate Cups (previous page); opposite: Fresh Raspberry Soup

MENU 3

(TO SERVE 4)

Gazpacho
with
Anchovy Bread

◇

Hot Lemon Chicken
with
Cold Herb Dressing
New Potatoes cooked in their
skins

◇

Pink Grapefruit Tart

GAZPACHO

1 thick slice wholemeal bread
900 ml / 1½ pints tomato juice
2 green peppers
1 cucumber
bunch of spring onions
450 g / 1 lb tomatoes
2 cloves garlic, crushed
salt and pepper
juice of ½ lemon
dash of Worcestershire sauce
some fresh basil, chopped

Cut the crusts off the bread, then break the slice up and put it into the food processor or liquidiser with half the tomato juice. Blend until smooth, put into a large bowl.

Cut the tops off the peppers and remove the pith and seeds from inside, chop the rest. Peel and dice the cucumber. Chop the onions. Peel and chop the tomatoes.

Put about a quarter of all the prepared vegetables in the liquidiser or food processor with the rest of the tomato juice, the garlic, seasoning and lemon juice. Blend until smooth and add to the first batch of tomato juice in the bowl. Add the Worcestershire sauce and basil and chill thoroughly.

Arrange the remaining finely chopped vegetables in a dish to serve with the soup.

NOTE: You can add some croûtons to serve with the soup if you like.

ANCHOVY BREAD

1 short wholemeal French loaf
75 g/3 oz butter
2 tablespoons anchovy essence
2 tablespoons chopped parsley
a few drops of lemon juice

Cut the loaf almost through into slices, leaving them attached at the base. Beat the butter until soft, then beat in the anchovy essence, parsley and lemon juice. Spread this between the slices, wrap the loaf in foil and bake in a moderately hot oven (200 C, 400 F, gas 6) for 10 to 15 minutes. Separate the slices, put them in a napkin-lined basket and serve hot.

HOT LEMON CHICKEN WITH COLD HERB DRESSING

1 large fresh roasting chicken (about 1.75 kg/4 lb in weight)
2–3 lemons
50 g/2 oz butter
DRESSING
a couple of handfuls of fresh herbs (the choice is yours) – chives, parsley, basil, mint (I use everything that's in the garden.)
50 ml/2 fl oz cider vinegar
1 tablespoon Dijon mustard
25 g/1 oz soft brown sugar
salt and pepper
juice of 1 lemon
250 ml/8 fl oz sunflower oil

Put the lemons inside the chicken. Put in a roasting tin and dot with the butter. Roast first on one side, then on the other in a moderately hot oven (190 C, 375 F, gas 5) for about 1½ hours, or until the chicken is cooked and the juices from the thickest part of the thigh run clear.

For the dressing, put the herbs in a food processor to chop, then add all the remaining ingredients; whizz them up to make a thick dressing.

Cut the chicken into serving pieces, arrange on a warm dish and pour over the cold dressing. Serve as soon as possible. The hot chicken and the cold dressing are an unusual combination.

GRAPEFRUIT TART

225 g/8 oz plain flour
175 g/6 oz butter
2 tablespoons caster sugar
1 egg yolk
FILLING
15 g/½ oz gelatine
3 tablespoons water
3 tablespoons caster sugar
300 ml/½ pint rosé wine
10–12 pink grapefruit
3 tablespoons redcurrant jelly, warmed

Sift the flour into a bowl and rub in the butter, then add the sugar and egg yolk and mix the ingredients together to form a soft dough (or do this in a food processor). Wrap the dough in cling film and chill for at least 15 minutes. Have ready a 25-cm/10-in loose-bottomed tart tin or dish. Roll out the pastry thinly and line the tin. Prick the base all over and place a piece of greaseproof paper in the flan case. Sprinkle in some dried peas or beans to weigh the paper down, then bake in a moderately hot oven (200 C, 400 F, gas 6) for 20 minutes. Remove the paper and peas or beans, put back in the oven for a further 5 to 10 minutes, or until it is cooked and lightly browned. Leave to cool.

Soften the gelatine in the water then dissolve over gentle heat. Add the sugar to the rosé and stir until it dissolves. Stir in the gelatine and set aside. Cut all the peel and pith off the grapefruit. Use a sharp knife to cut between the membranes and remove the segments. Add any juice to the gelatine mixture and chill until it is half set.

Brush the bottom of the flan with a layer of redcurrant jelly. Arrange the fruit in the pastry case. Spoon the rosé glaze over the grapefruit and chill until it sets completely. Serve the tart fairly soon after it is made – this cannot be made hours and hours in advance or the juice from the fruit will soften the pastry.

MENU 4

(TO SERVE 4)

Crudités with Dips

◇

Glazed Ham with Oranges
Damson Sauce
Lightly steamed Mange-tout
New Potatoes

◇

Coconut Cream Dessert

CRUDITÉS
WITH DIPS

APPLE MINT DIP
225 g/8 oz cream cheese
a few spring onions, chopped
2 dessert apples, peeled, cored and grated
4 tablespoons natural yogurt
a few sprigs of mint, chopped
PEANUT AND AVOCADO DIP
50 g/2 oz salted peanuts
$\frac{1}{2}$ small onion, chopped
2 ripe avocado pears, peeled, stoned and cubed
1 clove garlic, crushed
150 ml/$\frac{1}{4}$ pint soured cream
chilli powder to taste
CRUDITÉS
as many raw vegetables as possible
nasturtium leaves and flowers to garnish

Mix all the ingredients for the apple and mint dip and chill thoroughly. Put the peanuts and onion in a liquidiser or food processor and chop finely, then add all the remaining ingredients and process until smooth. Chill the second dip, not for too long or the avocado will discolour.

Prepare all the vegetables for the crudités. Arrange them on a large dish surrounding the bowls of dip. Add flowers to make it look decorative as well as edible.

GLAZED HAM WITH ORANGES

(Illustrated overleaf)

This is a simple traditional recipe but it is ideal for easy entertaining. The whole ham always looks nice and has the best flavour. It will, of course, serve about 30 people or leave you with plenty left over for other meals.

1 small whole gammon
250 ml/8 fl oz apple juice
6 tablespoons clear honey
generous pinch of ground cloves
1 teaspoon ground cinnamon
SPICED ORANGES
allow 1 orange per person
225 g/8 oz sugar
150 ml/¼ pint water
1 cinnamon stick
6 cloves
DAMSON SAUCE
450 g/1 lb damsons
2 tablespoons water
100 g/4 oz caster sugar
4 tablespoons port
GARNISH
rosemary
lemon balm

Soak the gammon for several hours (changing the water quite often). Calculate the cooking time at 25 minutes per 450 g/1 lb. If you have a large pan boil the gammon for 2 hours then roast it for the remaining time. Alternatively, roast the ham for the total cooking time. Put it in a roasting tin. Add the apple juice. Cover closely with foil and bake in a moderate oven (180 C, 350 F, gas 4) for the calculated time, or until the meat is cooked through. Carefully remove the skin and cut diamond shapes in the fat.

Mix the honey with the ground cloves, cinnamon, and the grated rind from two of the oranges. Brush this glaze over the gammon and put it back in the oven, uncovered, for a further 40 minutes, or until it is browned. Baste the ham several times with the honey and juices until cooked. Leave to cool completely (of course it can also be served hot).

To spice the oranges, cut off all the peel and pith and leave the fruit whole. Dissolve the sugar in the water with the cinnamon stick and the cloves added. When the sugar has dissolved, bring to the boil and cook until the syrup is just beginning to turn golden. Remove from the heat, pour over the oranges and leave to cool completely.

Halve and stone the damsons, then put them in a saucepan with the water and sugar. Heat slowly until the sugar melts, then continue to cook, stirring occasionally, for a few minutes. The damsons should be soft but not broken. Stir in the port and allow to cool before serving.

Place the ham on an extra large serving dish; arrange the oranges round it. Garnish with rosemary and lemon balm if it is going to be the centrepiece of a buffet.

NOTE: The ham tastes delicious if it is first boiled in apple juice. If serving the ham cold, make a large green salad with a herb dressing.

COCONUT CREAM DESSERT

175 g/6 oz plain flour
100 g/4 oz butter · 50 g/2 oz caster sugar
grated rind of 2 oranges
TOPPING
1 (198.45-g/7-oz) packet creamed coconut
150 ml/¼ pint boiling water
3 eggs, separated · 50 g/2 oz caster sugar
grated rind and juice of 2 limes
450 g/1 lb cream cheese
4 teaspoons gelatine · 4 tablespoons water
DECORATION
6–8 tablespoons long-thread coconut, toasted
150 ml/¼ pint double cream, whipped (optional)

Sift the flour into a bowl, then rub in the butter and stir in the sugar together with the orange rind. Press this into the base of a 23-cm/9-in springform tin and prick all over with a fork. Bake in a moderate oven (180 C, 350 F, gas 4) for 30 to 35 minutes. Remove from the oven and allow to cool.

Dissolve the creamed coconut in the boiling water, then set aside until cool. Beat the egg yolks with the sugar and lime rind until pale and creamy. Beat in the lime juice and cream cheese, then add the creamed coconut. Soften the gelatine in the water then dissolve over low heat. Allow to cool slightly, then stir the gelatine into the cream cheese mixture and leave until half set. Whisk the egg whites until they stand in stiff peaks. Fold them into the cheesecake mixture and turn it into the tin on top of the base. Chill.

Remove the sides of the tin and cover the top and sides of the cheesecake completely in the toasted coconut. If you want to gild the lily decorate with swirls of whipped cream.

Glazed Ham with Oranges (previous page)

MENU 5

(TO SERVE 4)

Pistachio Pasta

◇

Sole with Ginger Sauce

Fresh Spinach Salad

◇

Redcurrant and Blackcurrant
Pudding

PISTACHIO
PASTA

(Illustrated on page 119)

350 g / 12 oz pasta (whichever shapes you prefer)
bunch of spring onions
100 g / 4 oz pistachio nuts, chopped
2 bunches watercress
DRESSING
150 ml / ¼ pint olive oil (or sunflower oil if you
prefer)
1 clove garlic, crushed
large handful of basil, chopped
2 tablespoons mild wholegrain or Dijon mustard
(or use your favourite mustard)
3 tablespoons lemon juice
salt and pepper
150 ml / ¼ pint soured cream

Cook the pasta in plenty of boiling salted water for about 8 minutes, until it is just tender but not too soft. Drain and rinse immediately under cold water, then leave to drain thoroughly.

Chop the spring onions and mix them with the pistachio nuts in a large bowl. Set aside about half a bunch of watercress, then pick off the sprigs of the rest and put them in the bowl. Add the cooled pasta and toss well.

Put all the remaining ingredients (apart from the soured cream) in a food processor with the reserved watercress, with all the stalks and blend until smooth. Add the soured cream and pour this dressing over the salad.

SOLE WITH GINGER SAUCE

4 large sole fillets or 8 small ones
450 ml/¾ pint water
bay leaf
juice of ½ lemon
thinly pared rind of 1 lemon, cut into fine strips
40 g/1½ oz fresh root ginger, peeled and cut into very fine strips
1 teaspoon green peppercorns
salt and pepper
1 or 2 carrots, cut into very fine strips
2 egg yolks
4 tablespoons double cream

Lay the sole fillets in a large deep frying pan, fish kettle or flameproof casserole. Pour in the water, add the bay leaf, lemon juice, pared rind and ginger. Sprinkle the peppercorns into the pan and add a little seasoning. Bring slowly just to the boil, then reduce the heat and poach the fish very gently for about 5 minutes, or until it is cooked. Carefully lift the fish out of the cooking liquid, lay the fillets on warm plates and keep hot, covered.

Bring the cooking liquid quickly to the boil and boil rapidly to reduce it to half its original quantity. Remove the bay leaf and add the carrot strips, then cook for 1–2 minutes to soften them slightly. Stir the egg yolks into the cream, then add a little of the hot fish liquid. Stir well and reduce the heat under the pan, pour the cream mixture into the sauce, stirring all the time. Heat through (but do not let the sauce boil). Pour a little of the sauce over the fish and serve the rest separately.

FRESH SPINACH SALAD

about a dozen or so young spinach leaves
1 lambs lettuce
bunch of fresh young dandelion leaves
some marigold petals
DRESSING
several spring onions
a few sprigs of tarragon
3 tablespoons tarragon vinegar
about 150 ml/¼ pint sunflower oil
salt and pepper
generous pinch of sugar
generous pinch of mustard powder

Tear the spinach, lettuce and dandelion leaves into pieces and combine them in a bowl with the marigold petals and toss well. Put all the ingredients for the dressing in a screw-topped jar and shake until the mixture is smooth and well combined. Pour the dressing over the salad and toss just before you eat it.

EASY TOMATO SAUCE

When there are lots of ripe tomatoes in the greenhouse, try making a very simple sauce. Soften a large chopped onion in a mixture of butter and oil. Add crushed cloves of garlic (one or two, to taste) and lots of chopped tomatoes – you can add several pounds. Stir in a bay leaf and cover the pan, then simmer gently for about an hour. Blend until smooth in a liquidiser or food processor, then sieve to remove seeds. This freezes well and tastes great with cooked fresh pasta.

RED AND BLACK-CURRANT PUDDING

675 g / 1½ lb blackcurrants
175 g / 6 oz caster sugar
600 ml / 1 pint plus 4 tablespoons water
50 g / 2 oz gelatine
675 g / 1½ lb redcurrants
about 20–24 sponge fingers
DECORATION
currant leaves
flowers

String the blackcurrants, then put them in a saucepan with half the sugar and 300 ml/½ pint water. Poach gently until the fruit is tender. Soften half the gelatine in 2 tablespoons water, then stir into the hot fruit until completely dissolved. Prepare the redcurrants in exactly the same way.

Dip the sponge fingers briefly in some of the fruit juices, then use them to line an 18-cm/7-in round tin, or charlotte mould, or a large pudding basin. When the fruit is half set, put layers of both types of fruit into the basin and chill thoroughly until set.

To serve, turn the pudding out and surround with sprigs of currants and their leaves. Cut the pudding into slices – the layers look quite spectacular.

Pistachio Pasta (page 116)

SUMMER TABLE IDEAS

If flowers are difficult to come by or expensive, use single stemmed vases, each containing one rose, or freesia, or lily.

Decorate a basket of fruit (which could be your dessert) with flowers.

Place a wine glass filled with flowers and herbs in front of each guest.

Use an old sun hat turned upside down and put a bowl in the crown. Fill with flowers.

Fill a bowl with lemons and tuck some white daisies in between.

Take a large overblown cabbage, spread out the leaves as much as possible and fill with roses.

When eating outside, geraniums (especially the scented ones) left in their pots and lined up with candles look very pretty

Fill a large old jug with buttercups. Have a big bowl of roses mixed with rosemary. For a tea-party don't throw away a teapot just because the lid has broken – fill it with flowers and use to decorate your table.

Don't always feel you have to serve two or three courses. One delicious course, followed by fruit and cheese can be perfect.

When in doubt, go for simplicity.

Mix mint and lemon balm with flowers (lovely with snap dragons and sweet-peas).

Fill a shallow basket with pansies, or use lots of small vases filled with small flowers instead of one centrepiece.

Hunt in junk shops for old wash stand jugs and basins – the basins are perfect for flowers in the middle of the table (or for salad or fruit) and the jugs can be used for iced water, iced tea, or filled with long-stemmed flowers. Collect old plates – it doesn't matter if they don't match, in fact it's more interesting.

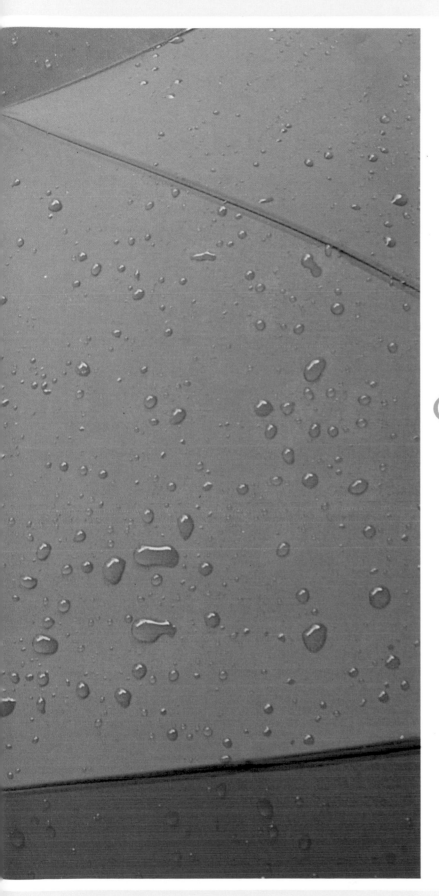

Rain Stopped Eating

SUNSHINE SOUP

(Illustrated on page 130)

SERVES 4 TO 6

450 g/1 lb carrots, chopped
1 large onion, chopped
25 g/1 oz butter
grated rind and juice of 2 oranges
600 ml/1 pint chicken stock
salt and pepper
glass of dry sherry
300 ml/½ pint single cream

Cook the carrots and onions in the butter for about 8 to 10 minutes, stirring frequently so that the onion softens. Add the orange rind and juice, then pour in the stock and bring to the boil. Cover and simmer for 30 minutes.

Blend the soup in a liquidiser and sprinkle in seasoning to taste with the sherry. Chill the soup thoroughly before stirring in the cream and serving.

Should the weather forecast prove to be disastrously wrong, and your friends are turning blue and asking for sweaters, serve this soup hot to warm them up. Heat the soup before adding the cream. Add the cream and continue to heat gently – but don't let it boil.

BIG RYE BISCUITS

MAKES 3

These are good to nibble while the barbecue is getting hot and they taste great with any dip.

175 g/6 oz rye flour
100 g/4 oz bran
50 g/2 oz rye flakes
1 teaspoon salt
15 g/½ oz butter
1 teaspoon caster sugar
1 (15-g/½-oz) sachet easy-blend yeast
300 ml/½ pint lukewarm water

Mix the rye flour, bran and rye flakes in a bowl. Add the salt and rub in the butter. Stir in the sugar and yeast, then work in the water to make a soft dough. Turn the dough out on to a work surface and knead it thoroughly for 10 minutes.

Divide the dough into three pieces. Roll each piece out very thinly into a big circle – about 25 cm/10 in across. Place these on greased baking trays and prick them all over with a fork. Leave to rise in a warm place for about an hour.

Bake the rye biscuits in a moderate oven (180 C, 350 F, gas 4) for 25 minutes. Cool on a wire rack.

MARINATED SEA BASS WITH FENNEL SAUCE

(Illustrated overleaf)

SERVES 4

Marinated fish dishes taste best when they are barbecued but this can be cooked in the oven.

1 large whole sea bass
300 ml/½ pint white wine
1 onion, sliced · bay leaf
a few black peppercorns
juice of 1 lemon
2 tablespoons dill or fennel
bunch of parsley · 25 g/1 oz butter
FENNEL SAUCE
1 small onion, finely chopped
1 large bulb of fennel
25 g/1 oz butter
3 tablespoons plain flour
150 ml/¼ pint dry white wine
150 ml/¼ pint fish stock
salt and pepper
grated rind and juice of 1 lemon
150 ml/¼ pint single cream

Ask your fishmonger to clean the fish for you. Rinse it with cold water and pat dry with absorbent kitchen paper. Place the fish in a large dish and pour the wine over. Add the onion slices, the bay leaf, peppercorns, lemon juice, dill or fennel and parsley. Scoop some of the mixture into the cavity of the fish. Marinate for several hours.

To cook the fish, drain off most of the wine, but keep the herbs and flavourings. Place on greased foil, dot with butter and tightly close the package. Cook on the barbecue, turning once, for about 40 to 50 minutes. Remove the skin, garnish with fresh dill.

While it is cooking make the sauce. Cut up the onion and fennel, put into the food processor and chop very finely, then cook in the butter until soft but not brown. Stir in the flour, cook for a minute, pour in the wine and stock, and bring to the boil. Add seasoning to taste and the lemon rind and juice. Simmer for 10 minutes. Stir in the cream and reheat gently but do not boil. Serve hot with the fish.

NOTE: If you like, serve the fish cold, with skin removed. Poach some redcurrants in a little orange juice and add sugar to taste. When cold, serve the redcurrant sauce with the fish.

BARBECUED SARDINES

Fresh sardines taste excellent when sprinkled with lemon juice and some freshly ground black pepper, then cooked straight on the barbecue. Turn the fish once or twice during cooking and serve with warm crusty bread. If you have to stay indoors, then cook the sardines under a hot grill.

CRUDITÉS

A basket of crudités is a must for barbecues – it will keep your guests' hunger pangs at bay while the food is cooking. Make all the crudités very fresh and crisp. Include cauliflower, carrot sticks, pieces of celery, sticks of courgette, wedges of apple, trimmed spring onions and button mushrooms. If you like you can add some chunks of cheese. Make a dip – just good mayonnaise flavoured with lots of chopped fresh herbs or garlic. Arrange in a basket.

BARBECUED TROUT WITH FENNEL AND LEMON

SERVES 4

4 fresh trout
several sprigs of fennel
2 lemons, one sliced
salt and pepper
sunflower oil for cooking

Ask the fishmonger to clean the trout for you, then rinse and dry them. Put a few sprigs of fennel and a few lemon slices in each fish. Season both inside and out with salt and pepper and brush with a little oil. Cook over the barbecue, keeping the rack well above the coals so that the fish does not cook too quickly on the outside. Turn the trout once during cooking, then serve hot with crusty French bread or Granary bread and a simple green salad. Quarter the remaining lemon to serve with the fish.

If the weather does not allow for a barbecue, then wrap each trout individually in foil and bake in a moderate oven (180 C, 350 F, gas 4) for about 45 minutes.

Marinated Sea Bass (previous page) shown with redcurrant sauce

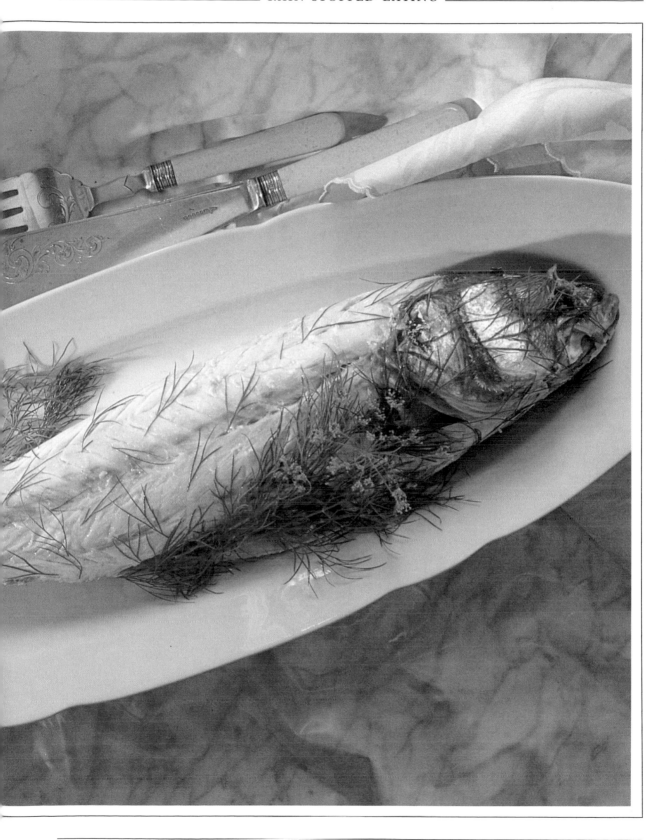

HONEYED CHICKEN

SERVES 4

4 chicken breast fillets
50 g/2 oz no-need-to-soak apricots, chopped
1 tablespoon clear honey
bunch of lemon balm, chopped
4 tablespoons olive oil
1 clove garlic, crushed (optional)
salt and pepper
2 tablespoons lemon juice

Trim the skin off the chicken and lay the fillets in a shallow dish. Mix all the remaining ingredients, then spread the mixture evenly over the chicken, cover and chill overnight or for several hours. Turn the chicken over after about 3 hours.

Cook the pieces of chicken over a hot barbecue, turning once, until well browned and cooked through. Alternatively grill the chicken. Serve with Red and Green Tomato Salad and hot crusty bread.

BARBECUE POPCORN

Put a mugful of popcorn on a double-thickness of cooking foil. Sprinkle with oil and wrap up securely, leaving the package very loose and large so that the popcorn has plenty of room to expand as it cooks. Put this on the barbecue and cook until the popping stops. Turn it into a bowl and stir in some melted butter. Alternatively, sprinkle with grated Parmesan cheese and chopped parsley or basil.

FILLED CHICORY LEAVES

SERVES 6 TO 8

2 (200-g/7-oz) cans tuna in oil
4 gherkins, chopped
1 tablespoon capers, chopped
½ teaspoon ground coriander
a few spring onions, chopped
1 generous tablespoon bean sprouts
salt and pepper
150 ml/¼ pint mayonnaise
2 heads chicory

Drain and flake the tuna, then add the gherkins, capers, coriander, spring onions and bean sprouts. Sprinkle in seasoning to taste and stir in the mayonnaise.

Separate the chicory leaves and pile a little of the tuna mixture on each leaf. Arrange the stuffed chicory leaves in a fan-shape.

NOTE: Try filling radicchio leaves instead of the chicory leaves. Use the same filling as above.

BARBECUED STUFFED PEPPERS

SERVES 4

4 medium yellow, green or red peppers
100 g/4 oz buckwheat
300 ml/½ pint boiling water
50 g/2 oz dried apricots, soaked and drained
1 dessert apple
50 g/2 oz hazelnuts or cashews, chopped and toasted
salt and pepper
1 onion, chopped
50 g/2 oz butter
1 clove garlic, crushed
a few sprigs of mint, chopped
4–5 tablespoons natural yogurt

Cut the tops off the peppers, then scoop out all the seeds and pith from inside to leave the shell whole. Reserve the lids. Cook the buckwheat in the boiling water for about 10 minutes or until all the liquid has been absorbed. Chop the apricots. Add the apricots to the buckwheat. Peel, core and dice the apple, add it to the buckwheat with the nuts and plenty of seasoning. Mix thoroughly.

Sauté the onion in the butter with the garlic until soft but not browned, then beat it into the buckwheat with all the pan juices and the mint. Lastly add the yogurt.

Divide the stuffing between the peppers, then replace the lids and wrap them tightly in foil. Cook the peppers on the barbecue for about 15 to 20 minutes, then serve them in their foil.

Bad weather? Then bake the peppers in a moderate oven (180 C, 350 F, gas 4) for about 40 minutes.

SKEWERED BREAD AND CHEESE

SERVES 4

16 thick slices wholemeal bread
225 g/8 oz Philadelphia cheese
8 tablespoons chutney (use your favourite)
salt and pepper
bunch of parsley, chopped
50 g/2 oz butter, melted

Cut the crusts off the bread if you wish. Beat the cheese with the chutney, seasoning and parsley, then use this to sandwich the bread slices together in pairs. Cut the sandwiches into cubes and thread these on to four long skewers. Brush the outside of the bread and cheese with melted butter, then cook on the barbecue, turning once, until brown and crisp.

The kebabs can be cooked under a hot grill instead. They are easy to make, good for a quick impromptu barbecue.

✻

BEETROOT
SALAD

SERVES 6

1 crisp Iceberg lettuce
450 g / 1 lb beetroot
grated rind and juice of 1 lemon
celery salt and pepper
6 tablespoons olive oil · pinch of sugar
150 ml / $\frac{1}{4}$ pint soured cream
bunch of chives, chopped

Put the sliced lettuce on a serving dish. Peel and grate the beetroot, put in a bowl and toss in the lemon rind and juice, celery salt and pepper to taste, oil and sugar. Pile the beetroot on top of the lettuce. Pour the soured cream over and top with the chives.

Opposite: Sunshine Soup (page 124) and Summer Chicken Hash Salad (page 133) also shown hot (above)

VEGETABLE KEBABS

SERVES 4

450 g/1 lb small new potatoes
1 large aubergine
1 green pepper
2 dessert apples
juice of ½ lemon
450 g/1 lb small onions (pickling onions)
8 bay leaves
150 ml/¼ pint olive oil
1 clove garlic, crushed
a few sprigs of rosemary, chopped
2 tablespoons chopped fresh marjoram or basil
generous dash of Worcestershire sauce
salt and pepper

BARBECUE SAUCE
1 onion, chopped
50 g/2 oz butter
1 tablespoon Dijon mustard
2 tablespoons tomato ketchup
generous dash of Tabasco sauce
1 tablespoon Worcestershire sauce
2 tablespoons demerara sugar
1 tablespoon plain flour
300 ml/½ pint red wine

SUMMER DRESSING
1 small carrot, chopped
50 g/2 oz frozen sweet corn
50 g/2 oz French beans, chopped
2 tablespoons olive oil
1 clove garlic, crushed
salt and pepper
bunch of spring onions, chopped
4 tomatoes, peeled, deseeded and chopped
1 tablespoon capers, chopped
a few sprigs of mint, chopped
4 tablespoons mayonnaise
150 ml/¼ pint soured cream

Scrub the potatoes and cook them for 5 minutes in boiling salted water. Drain thoroughly – they should be par-cooked, not completely tender. Trim the aubergine and cut it into chunks. Cut the stalk end off the pepper, remove the seeds and cut it into chunks. Core the apples and cut them into wedges. Sprinkle with the lemon juice. Thread the prepared vegetables, onions, bay leaves and apples on to eight skewers.

Mix the oil with the garlic, herbs, sauce and plenty of seasoning. Brush the kebabs with this mixture, then cook them on a barbecue for about 10 minutes each side. Baste the kebabs with more dressing as they cook. If the weather is too bad for barbecues, then put the kebabs under the grill.

For the sauces, cook the onion in the butter until soft. Stir in the mustard, ketchup, Tabasco, Worcestershire sauce, sugar and flour and cook for a minute. Pour in the wine and bring to the boil, then simmer until thickened. Add seasoning to taste and keep the sauce hot on the barbecue.

The summer sauce is a cool one: cook the carrot, corn and beans briefly in the oil with the garlic, then remove from the heat and stir in all the remaining ingredients. Chill lightly before serving. The two sauces make a pleasant contrast.

NOTE: Try using a mixture of cubed cooked ham, cubes of green or red pepper and dried apricots (you may have to soak these first) on the kebabs instead of the vegetables given above.

SUMMER CHICKEN HASH SALAD

(Illustrated on page 131)

SERVES 4 TO 6

450 g/1 lb small new potatoes, cooked
4 cooked chicken breasts
½ cucumber
2 red peppers
bunch of spring onions, chopped
handful of herbs of your choice, chopped
(tarragon or lemon balm are good)
DRESSING
150 ml/¼ pint mayonnaise
150 ml/¼ pint soured cream
salt and pepper
1 tablespoon toasted sesame seeds

If the potatoes are large then cut them into quarters or chunks. Cut the chicken into chunks, discarding any skin and bone. Roughly chop the cucumber. Cut the stalk ends off the peppers, remove any seeds and pith, then roughly chop.

Toss all the prepared ingredients together in a big bowl, adding the spring onions and herbs. Mix all the dressing ingredients and toss them into the salad so that it is well coated.

If the weather turns cold, this salad can be quickly transformed into a delicious chicken hash. Melt some butter or heat a little sunflower oil in large frying pan. Turn the salad (without the dressing) into the pan and press the ingredients down well with the back of a spatula. Cook until the underneath is lightly browned, dot with butter and cook under a hot grill until golden on top. Serve hot, cut into wedges, and offer the dressing with the hash, like a sauce.

RED AND GREEN TOMATO SALAD

SERVES 4

450 g/1 lb each red and green tomatoes
1 small onion, chopped
1 teaspoon caster sugar
2 tablespoons cider vinegar
150 ml/¼ pint olive oil
bunch of parsley, chopped
a few sprigs of mint
salt and pepper
1 (50-g/2-oz) can anchovies, chopped (optional)
chopped basil to garnish

Cut the tomatoes into slices, keeping both types separate. Arrange them in rings on a platter, then sprinkle with the onion. Mix all the remaining ingredients in a screw-topped jar and shake well. Pour this over the salad and leave to marinate in a cool place (not the refrigerator) for about an hour. Serve cool but not chilled. Garnish with chopped basil.

NOTE: Red tomato salad with cubed mozzarella cheese and roughly chopped basil is also delicious. Dress the salad with a squeeze of lemon and a little sunflower oil.

Another way of using up tomatoes – lay thick slices of red and green tomatoes in a lightly buttered dish. Season with salt and pepper, and a teaspoon of sugar. Pour over some cream and sprinkle with grated Cheddar cheese. Bake in the oven until the cheese is just turning brown.

SWEET PEA TART

SERVES 4 TO 6

If you are lucky enough to tire of fresh young peas out of the garden try this.

275 g / 10 oz wholemeal flour
salt and pepper
228 g / 8 oz butter or sunflower margarine
450 g / 1 lb cooked peas
chopped mint
large bunch of spring onions, chopped
300 ml / ½ pint single cream
3 large eggs, beaten

Put the flour in a bowl and add a generous pinch of salt, then rub in the butter or margarine and mix in only just enough cold water to make the pastry bind together. Alternatively, use a food processor.

Roll out the pastry and use to line a fairly deep 25-cm / 10-in flan dish. Prick the base all over with a fork and put a sheet of greaseproof paper in the flan. Sprinkle in some dried peas or beans and bake the pastry case in a moderately hot oven (200 C, 400 F, gas 6) for 15 minutes.

Remove the paper and beans, then put the cooked peas in the flan. Sprinkle with mint and the spring onions. Beat the cream into the eggs, adding plenty of seasoning. Pour this over the filling and bake in a moderate oven (180 C, 350 F, gas 4) for 30 minutes or until set and lightly browned on top. Serve hot or cold.

NOTE: I like to serve this with mange-tout salad.

Sweet Pea Tart with Red Tomato Salad with Mozzarella (page 133) and Minted Wheat Salad (page 105)

SPICED BARBECUED PEARS

SERVES 4

These will cook on the barbecue while you eat the main course.

4 large ripe pears
juice of 1 large lemon
8 tablespoons soft brown sugar
150 ml/¼ pint red wine
½ teaspoon each of ground cinnamon, ground ginger and ground cloves
several sprigs of lemon balm
50 g/2 oz butter

Peel the pears, leaving the stalks on. Sprinkle with lemon juice immediately to stop them turning brown, then place each pear on a large square of cooking foil. Lift the edges to contain the liquid.

Mix the sugar, wine and spices. Pour some of the wine mixture over each pear, add a sprig of lemon balm to each one and dot with butter. Wrap securely in the foil. Put on the barbecue for about 15 minutes. Serve with whipped cream.

If it's not barbecue weather cook the pears in a moderate oven (180c, 350f, gas 4) for about 20 minutes.

CLASSIC SUMMER PUDDING

SERVES 4 TO 6

1.25 kg/2½ lb fruit, including redcurrants and blackcurrants, blackberries and raspberries
175 g/6 oz caster sugar
grated rind and juice of 1 orange
grated rind of 1 lemon
4 tablespoons port
1 small wholemeal loaf (or white if you prefer)
whole fruit to decorate

Put the currants and any other fruit which needs cooking in a saucepan with the sugar, fruit rinds and juice. Poach gently until the juice runs and the fruit is softened. (You can also use strawberries, rhubarb, cherries, peaches and plums in summer pudding.)

Mix all the types of fruit together and stir in the port. Cut the crusts off the bread and slice it fairly thinly. Line a 1.15-litre/2-pint pudding basin with the bread, then put the fruit in and top with more bread. Cover and weight down, chill for several hours. Reserve any remaining fruit juice to pour over the pudding when it is turned out or whip the juice into double cream until thick.

Ease the blade of a palette knife between the pudding and the basin to loosen the pudding, then invert it on to a serving dish and pour over any reserved juice. Surround the pudding with lots of whole fruit – currants and soft fruit. Serve with whipped cream.

SPARKLING FRUIT JUICE

For a cool, long drink mix peach juice or passion fruit juice with sparkling white wine or champagne. Pour the fruit juice into tall glasses and add plenty of crushed ice. Try using some of the unusual fruit juices you can now buy – pear, guava, plum, mango and grape are some that taste delicious mixed in this way.

SUMMER MILK SHAKES

People often forget how delicious fresh fruit milk shakes are. Children love them. Blend chilled milk with enough honey to sweeten and whatever fruit happens to be available.

Midsummer
Madness

CELEBRATION DINNER

FOR 20

Cream Cheese and Vegetable Loaf

Fruit-filled Chicken

Chicken stuffed with Pistachios and Rice

Cool Parsley Sauce

Scrubbed Potato Salad

Lettuce Heart and Marigold Salad

Whole Cheese with Fresh Figs and Apricots

Home-made Oatcakes

Selection of Biscuits

Plum Pyramid or Apple and Mint Sorbet

A TIME GUIDE

Up to a week before
Make the meringues for the plum pyramid. Keep in airtight containers.
Make the sorbet and keep it in the freezer.
Buy the cheese.
Make the oatcakes and store them in an airtight container.

•

Two days before
Bone the chickens (or better still ask your butcher to do it). Prepare the stuffings, keep in the refrigerator.

•

The day before
Stuff and cook the chickens.
Prepare, but do not dress, the salads.
Make the dressings and keep in the refrigerator.
Make the cream cheese loaf.

•

On the morning
Do the flowers and decorations, put out candles.
Slice the chickens, cover and chill.
Turn out the cream cheese loaf, cover and chill.
Put out the cheese and prepare the fruit.

•

Two hours before
Lay the table.

•

One hour before
Dress the salads.
Assemble the meringue pyramid.

•

When the first course is served
Transfer the sorbet to the refrigerator.

CREAM CHEESE AND VEGETABLE LOAF

MAKE TWO OF THESE

675 g/1½ lb cream cheese
1 tablespoon chopped fresh basil
1 small onion, finely chopped
4 tablespoons mayonnaise
salt and pepper
225 g/8 oz asparagus, cooked until just tender
100 g/4 oz carrots, cut into fine strips and cooked
50 g/2 oz broken walnuts
100 g/4 oz French beans, cooked
large handful of parsley, chopped

Beat the cream cheese with the basil, onion, mayonnaise and seasoning to taste. The vegetables should be steamed so that they retain all their colour and texture.

Line a 1-kg/2-lb loaf tin with greaseproof paper and grease it with a little sunflower oil. Layer the cream cheese mixture with the vegetables, ending with a layer of cream cheese. Cover and chill for several hours, or overnight, until the mixture is firm.

Turn the loaf out and peel away the greaseproof paper, then cover it completely with chopped parsley, pressing the herb on with the blade of a knife. This is nice served with a tomato salad.

FRUIT-FILLED CHICKEN

(Illustrated overleaf)

If you have a good butcher, then ask him if he will bone the chickens for you.

1 fresh roasting chicken (about 1.75 kg/4 lb)
STUFFING
350 g/12 oz prunes, soaked overnight and stoned
8 oranges · 2 lemons
2 limes
100 g/4 oz wholemeal breadcrumbs
150 ml/¼ pint Madeira
salt and pepper

To bone the chicken, lay it breast side down and use a sharp knife to cut down the middle. Work on one side at a time and cut as close to the bones as possible removing all the meat. Take great care not to make any cuts in the skin and cut a fine sliver off the breastbone to prevent this. Once you have done one side, turn the chicken round and work down the second side.

Cut the prunes into pieces and put them in a bowl. Grate the rind from 2 oranges and add to the prunes, then remove all the peel and pith from the oranges. Use a small, sharp knife to cut between the membranes and remove the fruit segments. Add these to the prunes. Coarsely grate the rind from the lemons and limes and add to the stuffing with the breadcrumbs and Madeira. Mix well.

Put the stuffing in the chicken, fold the meat over and sew up the opening securely, to make a fairly long roll. Put this in a roasting tin and sprinkle with plenty of seasoning. Dot with the butter and roast in a moderately hot oven (190 C, 375 F, gas 5) for about 1¼ hours, or until the chicken is cooked and browned. Wrap the cooked chicken completely in foil and leave it to cool. To serve, slice as thinly as possible and arrange on a serving dish.

MARIGOLD
SALAD

10 lettuce hearts, halved
marigold petals
bunch of spring onions, chopped
300 ml/½ pint olive oil
2 cloves garlic, crushed
3 tablespoons mild mustard
50 ml/2 fl oz wine vinegar
2 teaspoons sugar

Toss the lettuce and petals in a large bowl. Put all the other ingredients into a liquidiser or food processor, then whizz them up until smooth. Pour over the salad at the last minute.

Above: Fruit-filled Chicken (previous page) and
Chicken Stuffed with Pistachios and Rice (page 144);
opposite: Marigold Salad

CHICKEN STUFFED WITH PISTACHIOS AND RICE

(Illustrated on previous page)

1 large roasting chicken (about 1.75 kg/4 lb in weight)
STUFFING
225 g/8 oz long-grain brown rice
100 g/4 oz pistachio nuts, chopped
bunch of spring onions
1 large onion, chopped
1 clove garlic, crushed
50 g/2 oz butter
bunch of watercress, finely chopped
salt and pepper
2 tablespoons double cream
a few sprigs of tarragon, chopped
small cup of parsley, chopped
2 tablespoons dry sherry

Bone the chicken (see page 141) or ask your butcher to do this for you.

Cook the brown rice in boiling salted water. Mix the nuts with the rice, add the spring onions. Cook the chopped onion with the garlic in the butter until soft, then add to the stuffing with the watercress, plenty of seasoning, the cream and the herbs. Stir in the sherry and use this stuffing to fill the chicken as for the previous recipe.

Roast in a moderately hot oven (190 C, 375 F, gas 5) for about 1¼ hours, then wrap in foil until cool.

COOL PARSLEY SAUCE

several handfuls of parsley, chopped
2 cloves garlic, crushed
grated rind and juice of 2 lemons
salt and pepper
600 ml/1 pint mayonnaise
300 ml/½ pint soured cream

Mix all the ingredients together, then pour into a serving dish and chill thoroughly before serving.

SCRUBBED POTATO SALAD

2.25 kg/5 lb small new potatoes
2 bunches spring onions
450 g/1 lb shelled peas, cooked
bunch of fresh basil or marjoram, chopped
bunch of mint, chopped
300 ml/½ pint olive oil
50 ml/2 fl oz cider vinegar
1 clove garlic, crushed
2 teaspoons caster sugar
1 tablespoon mild wholegrain mustard

Scrub the potatoes and cook them in boiling salted water until tender – about 10 minutes. Drain thoroughly.

Chop the onions and sprinkle them over the hot potatoes, adding the peas and herbs. Put the remaining ingredients in a liquidiser or food processor and whizz them up until thoroughly combined. Pour this dressing over and toss the potatoes in it to coat them all completely. Cool then chill the salad.

BRIE WITH FIGS AND APRICOTS

Buy one ripe brie from a good cheese shop. Make sure that it is in tip-top condition because it is not possible to ripen a poor cheese at home. Have fresh apricots and figs to serve with the cheese and offer a selection of plain biscuits, some of them home-made. Why not make the oatcakes?

Arrange on a basket, with leaves and flowers to decorate.

OATCAKES

MAKE TWO LOTS

100 g/4 oz plain flour
100 g/4 oz medium oatmeal
salt
75 g/3 oz butter
1 tablespoon caster sugar
1 egg

Put the flour, oatmeal and a generous pinch of salt in the food processor with the butter and sugar. Whizz the ingredients until the butter is blended in, then add the egg and mix until a dough is formed.

Turn this out on to a floured board and roll it out very thinly. Use a plain biscuit cutter to cut out the biscuits, then put them on a greased baking tray and bake in a moderate oven (180 C, 350 F, gas 4) for about 15 to 20 minutes. Leave the oatcakes on the trays for a few minutes, then transfer them to wire racks to cool completely.

APPLE AND MINT SORBET

MAKE THREE LOTS

600 ml/1 pint apple juice
small bunch of mint (apple mint if you have it), chopped
100 g/4 oz sugar
2 egg whites

Pour the apple juice into a saucepan and add the mint. Stir in the sugar and heat gently, still stirring, until all the sugar has dissolved. Leave to cool, then pour the syrup into a freezer container or ice cream maker.

Freeze until half frozen, then remove and whisk thoroughly to break down all the ice crystals. Whisk the egg whites until they are stiff, fold them into the slushy mixture and put it back in the freezer. Whisk the water ice another three times during freezing, to break down the crystals and produce a smooth result.

When the mixture is smooth, leave it to freeze until hard. Put the water ice in the refrigerator for about 20 minutes before scooping it out of the container. Use an ice cream scoop and place in a flower ice-bowl or on to a large glass dish decorated with sprigs of mint.

PLUM PYRAMID

This is easier to handle if you make the meringue mixture in two batches. Use half to make the largest and smallest meringue rounds, then use the second batch to make the two middle rounds.

10 egg whites
575 g / 1¼ lb caster sugar
FILLING
1.5 kg / 3 lb plums
50 g / 2 oz sugar
4 tablespoons water
1.15 litres / 2 pints double cream
50 ml / 2 fl oz brandy or Kirsch

Whisk the egg whites until they stand in stiff peaks, then gradually whisk in the sugar, adding it slowly and whisking with an electric mixer on the highest speed. When all the sugar is incorporated, continue whisking hard until the meringue is very glossy and stiff.

Line four baking trays with non-stick cooking parchment. Draw a circle on each – one 25 cm/10 in, one 20 cm/8 in, one 15 cm/6 in, and one 10 cm/4 in. Spread the meringue thickly in these circles, then dry out in a very cool oven (110 C, 225 F, gas ¼), leaving the oven door slightly ajar. The meringues will take about 5 hours to dry out.

For the filling, peel and halve the plums, put them in a pan with the sugar and water, then poach gently until the juice runs and the fruit is just soft but still whole. Leave to cool, then strain the plums, reserving the syrup. Whip the cream with the plum syrup and the brandy or Kirsch, then fold in the fruit. Stack the meringue rounds, sandwiching them together with the plum cream. Spread the remaining cream on top.

LATE NIGHT CELEBRATION

FOR 20

Jellied Vegetable Mould
Cheese and Nut Stick

◇

Chocolate Fudge Cake

◇

Iced Herb Tea

A TIME GUIDE

The day before
Make the vegetable mould.
Make the fudge cake.
Make the nut bread.

●

On the day, well in advance
Decorate the cake.
Make the herb tea and chill.
Turn out the vegetable mould.
Prepare the table.

●

As late as you can leave it
Garnish the mould, then chill.

●

Just before you eat
Remove the vegetable mould from the refrigerator.
Put the bread in the oven.

JELLIED VEGETABLE MOULD

(Illustrated overleaf)

1 large cauliflower
4–6 large carrots
225 g/8 oz shelled fresh peas
2 red peppers
1 small head celery
2 small red onions
packet of bean sprouts
1 (411-g/14½-oz) can beef consommé
150 ml/¼ pint dry sherry
15 g/½ oz gelatine
450 ml/¾ pint hot water
large bunch of parsley, chopped
handful of small basil leaves
TO SERVE
300 ml/½ pint mayonnaise
4 tablespoons soured cream
2 tablespoons capers, chopped
juice of ½ lemon
salt and pepper

Cook the cauliflower and carrots by steaming them separately for 5 to 10 minutes so that they are only *just* tender. Cook the peas in boiling water for 2 minutes, drain thoroughly. Cut the tops off the peppers, remove the seeds and chop. Slice the celery. Thinly slice the onions. Blanch the pepper and celery together in boiling water for 2 minutes, then drain thoroughly. Wash and dry the bean sprouts. Mix or layer all these vegetables in a glass serving bowl, packing them in well.

Mix the consommé with the sherry. Soften the gelatine in a little cold water, then dissolve over low heat. Stir the gelatine and hot water into the consommé mixture. Sprinkle the parsley and basil over the vegetables and pour in the consommé, then chill thoroughly.

For the sauce, mix the mayonnaise with the cream, capers, lemon juice and seasoning.

CHEESE AND NUT STICK

1 large, long wholemeal French loaf
225 g/8 oz cream cheese
1 large clove garlic, crushed
some mixed fresh herbs
225 g/8 oz mixed nuts (include at least 50 g/2 oz salted peanuts)
50 g/2 oz butter

Cut the loaf horizontally in half, then place the halves on pieces of cooking foil. Beat the cream cheese with the garlic. Add the herbs to the cheese with seasoning and beat well. Spread this over the cut bread, making a thick, even layer.

Chop the nuts, then press them on top of the cream cheese mixture and dot with the butter. Wrap the loaves completely in foil and bake in a hot oven (220 C, 425 F, gas 7) for 15 minutes. Serve cut into slices – best hot or warm.

ICED HERB TEA

Make your favourite herb tea (Green Gunpowder iced tea or Lapsang Souchong tea is nice). Add a little sugar, then cool and strain. Chill the tea thoroughly before serving with lots of ice, slices of lemon and small sprigs of mint.

CHOCOLATE FUDGE CAKE

MAKE TWO OF THESE

225 g/8 oz butter
225 g/8 oz dark soft brown sugar
3 eggs, lightly beaten
1 (400-g/14.1-oz) can condensed milk
25 g/1 oz cocoa
4–5 tablespoons boiling water
275 g/10 oz plain flour
2 teaspoons baking powder
½ teaspoon bicarbonate of soda
DECORATION
150 ml/¼ pint double cream
frosted rose petals and violets

Cream the butter with the sugar until very soft. Beat in the eggs and condensed milk. Dissolve the cocoa in the boiling water, then beat it into the mixture.

Sift the flour with the baking powder and the bicarbonate of soda, then fold this into the mixture. Line and grease a 20–cm/8-in deep cake tin and turn the mixture into it. Bake the cake in a moderate oven (180 C, 350 F, gas 4) for 1¼ to 1½ hours. Leave the cake in the tin for a few minutes, then turn out on to a wire rack to cool.

Whip the cream until it stands in soft peaks, then swirl over the top of the cake. Add crystallised flowers.

Jellied Vegetable Mould (previous page)

BRUNCH PARTY

FOR 20

Smoked Trout Mousse

◇

Fresh Vegetable Gratin
Watercress Salad

◇

Lemon Jelly

◇

Coffee

A TIME GUIDE

The day before
Make the mousse in lemons and chill.
Prepare the gratin ready to put in the
oven, then chill.
Make the lemon jelly and chill.

●

Two hours before
Turn out the jelly.
Lay the table.

●

One hour before
Prepare everything for coffee.
Garnish the mousse in lemons.

●

About 45 minutes before
Prepare the oven for the gratin,
ready to put it in just before serving
the first course.
If this is being served outside, find a
shady spot and put food out at the last
minute. Put out a basket of sun hats
for guests.

SMOKED TROUT MOUSSE

(Illustrated overleaf)

For a party of twenty make three lots of this rather than trying to prepare vast quantities all at once. The quantities given here are enough to fill about six or eight lemons. Remember to save all the juice from the lemons to make the dessert jelly.

3 whole smoked trout
150 ml/¼ pint mayonnaise
8 lemons
2 eggs, separated
salt and pepper
15 g/½ oz gelatine
3 tablespoons water
about 6 nasturtium flowers or leaves

Skin, bone and flake the smoked trout then put it in a food processor or liquidiser with the mayonnaise, the grated rind of 1 lemon, the egg yolks, seasoning to taste and a little lemon juice. Process until smooth.

Dissolve the gelatine in the water. Roughly chop the nasturtium leaves and add them to the mousse, then stir in the gelatine. Whisk the egg whites until stiff, fold these into the mousse and chill until it just begins to set. Meanwhile, carefully cut the tops off the remaining lemons and squeeze out all the juice. Scrape out the lemon shells, taking care not to make any holes in them. Cut a sliver off the base of each lemon so that they stand up neatly.

Spoon the mousse into the lemons, piling it up in the middle. Use old egg boxes to support the lemons while you do this, put them in the refrigerator so that they are thoroughly chilled and the mousse is set before serving. Serve on saucers covered with more leaves.

LEMON JELLY

2.25 litres/4 pints water
75 g/3 oz gelatine
4 vanilla pods
a few sprigs of lemon balm
juice of 20 lemons (reserved from making the mousse)
grated rind of 4 lemons
450 g/1 lb sugar
150 ml/¼ pint Madeira

Pour about 150 ml/¼ pint of the water on to the gelatine and set aside. Gently heat the rest of the water with the split vanilla pods and lemon balm until it reaches boiling point. Leave to cool, strain and pour back into the pan.

Add the lemon juice and rind, and sugar to the water and heat until the sugar dissolves. Leave to cool. Dissolve the gelatine in the water over low heat. Stir it into the lemon mixture. Add the Madeira and pour into three 1.75-litre/3-pint moulds. Chill until set, then turn out and decorate with sprigs of lemon balm and flowers.

WATERCRESS SALAD

10 bunches watercress
2 bunches spring onions
1 head curly endive, trimmed and roughly shredded
DRESSING
150 ml/¼ pint olive oil
4 tablespoons red wine vinegar
2 tablespoons honey
2 tablespoons Worcestershire sauce
grated rind and juice of 2 oranges

Trim the watercress, then put it in a big bowl with the chopped spring onions and the endive. Mix thoroughly. Shake all the dressing ingredients together in a large screw-topped jar, then pour this over the salad just before it is served.

Above: Smoked Trout Mousse (page 153); opposite: Fresh Vegetable Gratin (overleaf)

FRESH VEGETABLE GRATIN

(Illustrated on previous page)

Use all the fresh vegetables you have in the garden, or the freshest you can buy in the shops for this gratin – make it full of colour.

1 cauliflower
450 g / 1 lb small onions (pickling onions)
450 g / 1 lb baby carrots
450 g / 1 lb French beans
450 g / 1 lb small new potatoes
450 g / 1 lb small tomatoes, halved
450 g / 1 lb shelled fresh peas and mange-tout peas
(Use any vegetables you particularly like, celery, chicory, artichoke bottoms, courgettes, peppers or aubergines are all excellent in this dish. The above is just to give you a guide.)
SAUCE
1 large onion, chopped
50 g / 2 oz butter
50 g / 2 oz plain flour
salt and pepper
300 ml / $\frac{1}{2}$ pint dry white wine
300 ml / $\frac{1}{2}$ pint milk
freshly grated nutmeg
175 g / 6 oz Cheddar cheese, grated
300 ml / $\frac{1}{2}$ pint double cream
2 eggs, beaten
large bunch of parsley, chopped

Prepare the vegetables according to their type, breaking the cauliflower into pieces, trimming and scraping the root vegetables, trimming beans and mange-tout and cutting any large vegetables into chunks. Steam the vegetables very briefly so that they are still crisp and fresh.

Put the vegetables in one or two ovenproof dishes. To make the sauce, cook the onion in the butter until it is soft but not browned. Stir in the flour and seasoning, then gradually add the wine and the milk. Bring to the boil, stirring all the time, and cook for 2 minutes. Remove the pan from the heat and stir in plenty of nutmeg and most of the cheese, saving some to sprinkle over the top. When the cheese has melted, beat in the cream and eggs, then add the parsley. Taste the sauce to make sure that it is well seasoned, then pour it over the vegetables.

Sprinkle the reserved cheese over the gratin and cook in a moderately hot oven (200 C, 400 F, gas 6) for about 30 minutes, until golden brown and bubbling. Serve as soon as possible.

Large summer parties can be made very special by making your table (or tables) look as beautiful as possible – use lots of candles and flowers, music and imagination.

ICE BOWLS

You will need some small flowers (pansies, for example) or petals, a few sprigs of fern or a few delicate leaves; boiled, cooled water and two freezerproof bowls (china, tough glass or plastic). One should hold twice the capacity of the other.

Half fill the larger bowl with cooled boiled water, then lower in the smaller one. Put stones or ice-cubes into the smaller bowl until the rims of both are level. Float the smaller one into the centre, with about 2.5 cm/1 in of water between the bowls. Use tape to hold the bowls in position. Freeze for about 10 minutes.

Using a skewer or thin-bladed knife, poke flowers or petals, and bits of greenery in between the bowls. Replace the bowls in the freezer and leave for 24 hours. To use the ice bowl, remove the tape and the stones or ice cubes. Fill the small bowl with lukewarm water and gently twist it until it is free. Carefully lift the small bowl away from the ice. Dip the larger bowl in luke-warm water until the ice bowl can be loosened and lifted out. Replace the ice bowl in the freezer until ready to serve.

SUMMER FRUITS

During the summer, as each berry comes into season layer them in a large stoneware jar (with a tight-fitting lid) with alcohol and brown sugar. Then at the end of the season, making sure the fruit is covered in liquid, put in a layer of brown sugar and seal the jar. Open during the winter – use as a sauce or mix with cream or yogurt. The ways to use it are numerous and it will remind you of those delicious fruits of summer.

WEEKEND GUESTS

Think of all the things you would love to find if you were staying with someone, then do it for your guests.

REMINDER LIST

Radio

Alarm clock

Up-to-date magazines

A recent novel

A basket of fruit (and perhaps some home-made biscuits)

Hair dryer

Hair rollers

Electric blanket

Bath essence, and bath wrap

And some flowers, and perhaps breakfast in bed

FROSTED FLOWERS

Very lightly whisk an egg white with a few drops of water. Use a small soft paint brush to brush the egg white all over flowers or petals, then dip in caster sugar to coat them completely. Shake off any excess sugar and leave the flowers to dry on absorbent kitchen paper.

INDEX